Celebrate WITH
BAKING

Celebrate WITH BAKING

SWEETS and TREATS for EVERY SPECIAL OCCASION

MALEK BINNS

PHOTOGRAPHY BY KATE SEARS

ROCKRIDGE
PRESS

Interior and Cover Designer: Patricia Fabricant
Art Producer: Michael Hardgrove
Editor: Rebecca Markley
Production Editor: Emily Sheehan

Photography © 2020 Kate Sears. Food styling by Liza Jernow.

ISBN: Print 978-1-64611-770-3 | eBook 978-1-64611-771-0

R0

To my mother and grandmother,
as a token of my gratitude
for being my inspirations and
molding my baking journey.

*White Chocolate Raspberry
Cheesecake, page 44*

CONTENTS

Homemade
Pretzels, page 160

INTRODUCTION

Baking is my SUPERPOWER. My apron is my CAPE.

Hello, everyone, and thank you for taking the time to pick up my very first cookbook! For those of you who don't know me, my name is Malek Binns, owner and operator of FROSTED by Malek Binns and its brother company, Sprinkled by Malek. I started my baking journey at the tender age of 13 and have always loved being in the kitchen—and loved that you can make anything with your hands and eat it, too! One of my many favorite things about baking is creating memorable desserts for those special occasions, and, like most bakers, I enjoy being creative and bringing joy to my customers when I make the cake or cookies of their dreams!

In one's lifetime, there are so many occasions that call for celebration, so many that mark a transitional period and require "that one special thing" to make it complete. Think about it: What do a birthday party, a graduation party, and a wedding reception have in common (other than dancing, of course)? They're all celebrated with a dessert that brings everyone together! The flavors and decorations may change throughout the years, but the scene stays the same.

Before we get started, ask yourself this question: What does the term "baking" mean to me? For me, baking is a productive form of self-expression and communication. I create what I want to create, however simple or magnificent that baked good may be. When I worked a 9-to-5 job in a corporate environment, coming home and baking cakes (even from a boxed mix) helped me relax and unwind. It simply felt like me. In a job where I didn't have much creative freedom, baking kept me fulfilled and energized. Baking is therapy.

It's a double whammy of awesomeness—baking makes me happy, and baked goods make *everyone* happy. Spreading joy is immensely powerful.

Take this book as a guide that you can use to make delicious, wonderful desserts for special occasions for the entire year. It is designed to inspire you to go into the kitchen and learn how to bake and, more importantly, to get the creative juices flowing and create something that only you can make. This book is full of detailed recipes and tips for all levels, beginner to advanced, and they are designed to be cost-effective.

My goal with every recipe is that it's easy to follow, tastes delicious, and has something in there that makes you smile. Please take a look around and let the book influence you the way it has me. Then, of course, don't forget to share and tag me on social media! @frostedbymalekbinns

Stay sweet!

Chapter 1
GET READY!

As we get started, it's important to understand that baking is not only a fun activity, but it is also a science experiment. You cannot just throw anything and everything into a bowl, slap it in the oven, and expect a delicious dessert to pop out. (If only it were that easy!) I cannot stress enough how important it is to prepare yourself beforehand to learn the basics of baking.

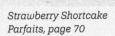

Strawberry Shortcake Parfaits, page 70

KITCHEN ESSENTIALS

I have been baking for years, and I use so many tools and ingredients that it's hard to keep count. While you don't need a fully stocked pastry kitchen, I want to share some of my favorites with you. Whether you're baking a batch of cookies or decorating a cake, the following are must-haves that every home baker should acquire before getting started.

TOOLS

Baking Pans: A set of baking pans can make or break your bake. If you prefer a lighter crust when baking, stick to light or glass pans, as the heat is reflected. Dark pans absorb the heat, which results in a darker crust. No worries if you have a dark pan, though. Just reduce your oven temperature by 25 degrees so that your bakes don't brown too fast. Brand isn't a major factor here, but it's worth mentioning that Fat Daddio's and Wilton are great options to work with.

- **Bundt Pan:** This pan is perfect for my Lemon-Lime Pound Cake (page 134) and Eggnog Bundt Cake (page 124). Bundt pans can come in a variety of styles, shapes, and ridges, so take your pick.

- **Baking Sheet:** A flat, rectangular metal pan with no edge for baking cookies.

- **Loaf Pan:** The standard-size loaf pan is 8½ by 4½ by 2½ inches. Used for baking traditional bread loaves.

- **Muffin Tin:** A baking pan with molds used to make muffins and cupcakes. The 12-cup pan is standard.

- **Rectangular Cake Pan:** A traditional sheet pan, known as the quarter sheet pan, that is used for sheet cakes and thick brownies and bars. A standard size—and the size most often used in this book—is 13 by 9 by 2 inches.

- **Round Pan:** You will only need either 8- or 9-inch round pans for the recipes in this book. The traditional depth is 2 inches, although I prefer 3-inch pans for thicker cakes. Many cake recipes in this book will call for multiple layers, so have multiple pans available for when you go to make those.

Cookie Cutters: For this book, we'll use basic shapes, square and triangle cookie cutters. You can buy metal and plastics ones at your local grocery store, or check out your local craft or cake supply store if you want something more elaborate. Starting a cookie cutter collection is a nice hobby. Some of my favorite shops are Crumbs Cutters, SheyB Designs, KaleidaCuts, and Cut It Out Cutters, which sells a plaque cutter named after yours truly!

Cooling Rack: Used to allow air to circulate freely around your bake, which promotes even cooling. It prevents baked goods from building condensation and steam, which can make them wet and soggy.

Decorating Bags and Tips: Commonly used for decorating cakes, cupcakes, and other baked goods but also used for piping dough (think eclairs or churros). You can choose disposable plastic bags—perfect for writing and decorating—or reusable bags made out of nylon, silicone, cotton, or canvas that are perfect for icing a cake. There are thousands of piping tips out there, including some that require a coupler (a tool used to hold a decorating tip on the end of a bag), which makes it easy to switch tips on a single bag. Make sure to do a little research to decide the best type of bag and tips for your needs. My go-to decorating bags and tips are from Ateco and Borderlands Bakery.

Electric Mixer: This is your true baking assistant. Mixers will do all the muscle work for you—unless you want to build some gains!—and are used to combine ingredients as well as whip. There are two types:

- **Hand Mixer:** A small handheld "assistant" that is used to combine ingredients. It comes with a pair of beaters that are removable for easy cleanup. Some brands carry different kinds of beaters that can be used to stir, beat, whip, and knead. This is an inexpensive option if you would like to promote yourself from mixing with a spoon.

- **Stand Mixer:** I like to call this the Ferrari of mixers. They can be pricey, but I believe one is worth the cost, especially if you bake often. This is a true assistant that will allow you to do your job hands-free. KitchenAid is the most well-known brand.

Spatulas: Used when working with batter, frosting, or sauces.

- **Offset Spatula:** Used to frost a cake, creating a pristine, smooth finish. The long and sturdy blade is perfect for scooping and spreading frosting, especially in those places that are hard to reach. You can also use it to transfer a cake from the cooling rack to a cake board or stand.

- **Rubber Spatula:** Used to fold or blend batters or to scrape the sides of the bowl without damaging it.

- **Silicone (Heatproof) Spatula:** Used to stir hot foods on the stove, like the cherry filling in the Black Friday Black Forest Cake (page 90).

INGREDIENTS

Chemical Leaveners: Used to help release gas to enhance quality in baked goods.

- **Baking Powder:** Contains sodium bicarbonate (baking soda) plus a starch (cornstarch or cream of tartar) to prevent lumps. Baking powder can be a double-acting agent, at first when in contact with liquid and again when in contact with heat.

- **Baking Soda:** This is sodium bicarbonate—one of the most widely used leaveners in baking. When an acid or moisture ingredient is active, such as vinegar, buttermilk, sour cream, or molasses, the carbon dioxide gas bubbles expand under heat, causing baked goods to expand or rise.

Cocoa Powder: Made from the remains of chocolate liquor, pressed to remove 75 percent of the cocoa butter. It tastes very bitter but gives a smooth chocolate flavor. It is used for brownies, cookies, cakes, and frostings.

Extracts: Used to add tremendous flavor to baked goods. Vanilla is the most common extract, created from vanilla beans and an alcohol-based mixture that ferments for months to get that authentic flavor. When purchasing vanilla, make sure it says "natural" or "pure" to ensure full flavor.

Fat: Gives flavor, assists with leavening, adds moistness and richness, and increases the shelf life of baked goods.

- **Butter:** The most common ingredient in baking, made up of 80 percent fat, 15 percent water, and 5 percent milk. My recipes, unless otherwise specified, call for unsalted butter, which is preferred so that your bakes are not too salty.

- **Vegetable Shortening:** Pure fat used in many recipes to create a flaky texture, especially in piecrusts and biscuits.

Flour: Provides the foundation, crumb, and texture in almost every baked good. There are many types of flour, but the most common type is unbleached all-purpose flour, which I use for most of the recipes in this book.

Sugar: Adds sweetness and flavor and plays other essential roles in recipes, as well. It can create tenderness, help leaven breads while baking, and keep baked goods soft and moist.

- **Brown Sugar:** Basically white, or granulated, sugar combined with molasses—a thick brown syrup that is produced and removed from creating raw sugar—to give it a richer caramel color and flavor plus moisture. There are two types: light and dark. The difference is simply the amount of molasses added. Note that it is very important to keep brown sugar in a sealed, airtight container to prevent dehydration. If the sugar dehydrates or becomes hard, you can revive it: Seal the hardened sugar in an airtight container with a slice of sandwich bread for a few hours so that the molasses can suck up the moisture.

- **Confectioners' Sugar:** A very finely ground sugar that you can dust on finished desserts and use to make frostings and glazes.

- **Granulated Sugar (white sugar):** Refined and made from cane sugar.

DECORATIONS

Candies: Candy is an easy and perfect way to decorate desserts! Add jelly beans to springtime cupcakes or candy corn to autumn cookies, or get wild and fill a cake with candy-coated chocolates (see the Confetti Rainbow Cake tip, page 140). The possibilities are endless, so let your imagination run wild.

Edible Luster Dust: A type of edible powder used in cake decorating. You can use it to add color to icings, frostings, and glazes. You can apply it dry with a brush or add vodka to make a paste for matte coverage. There are also metallic shades that can add a beautiful sparkle to your treats. My favorite brand is The Sugar Art Inc. They produce the best color and metallic dusts, which are FDA-approved. Try their DiamonDust—it's edible glitter!

Food Coloring: Edible dye that consists of chemicals used to add color to food. There are two types: liquid and gel. I prefer gel because it is more concentrated and won't thin out batter due to its thicker consistency. Any brand will do, but my favorite product is AmeriColor. They make very concentrated gel paste food coloring and thousands of colors to choose from. They also sell bundles—like the 12-count Student Kit for those who want to learn about color or a 70-count Heavenly Seventy Kit if you want to go all in.

Sanding Sugar: Edible sparkle for your decorating needs. You can purchase it inexpensively at the local grocery or cake supply store or make your own! Put ½ cup of granulated sugar in a plastic zip-top bag. Add food coloring one drop at a time and shake until combined and the desired color is achieved. If the mixture becomes sticky, add ¼ teaspoon of cornstarch to dry it out and prevent lumps. Use it right away or store in an airtight container for up to one year.

Sprinkles a.k.a. Jimmies: What can't you do with sprinkles? You can place them on top of anything with frosting, add them to batters and doughs—like my Sprinkledoodles cookies (page 146)—or add them to ice cream just to make it that much more special. There is a wide variety of colors, shapes, and sizes that you can choose from. My recommendation is my company, Frosted by Malek. I create custom mixes for your special event.

BAKING TERMINOLOGY

As you've learned, baking is all about the details, and many terms are used that have specific meanings to help your bakes be as perfect as possible. For example, "combine" does not mean the same thing as "fold," which does not mean the same thing as "beat." Don't worry, though—I've broken down the meanings so that you'll be ready from the get-go.

Beat: The process of briskly mixing or whipping with a spoon, fork, or mixer to combine ingredients to a smooth texture.

Combine: To blend two or more ingredients using a spoon, stand mixer, or food processer.

Cream: To beat a fat, such as butter or shortening, with sugar to ensure a light and fluffy mixture. This process helps make baked products larger in volume, softer in consistency, and pale in color.

Ferment: A chemical reaction through which yeast releases carbon dioxide, causing the dough to expand and rise.

Fold: A technique used to combine two mixtures in a very gentle way. When folding, a rubber spatula should be used.

Knead: To mix dough by hand, using methods of stretching, pushing, and folding in order to build gluten in many yeast breads.

Sift: The process of passing dry ingredients through a sieve to break up lumps. This method is performed before combining to achieve a smooth consistency.

Stir: To mix two or more ingredients in a circular motion until combined using a kitchen utensil/tool.

Whisk: Using a whisk or fork to mix very quickly so that air is incorporated.

HELPFUL HOW-TOS

In the previous section, you learned how baking is its own science. Now it's time for the fun part! Let's get our hands and spatulas dirty and learn some basic techniques that every baker should know. From measuring ingredients to decorating a cake, these techniques are easy and helpful—and, if performed properly, will make your baking a breeze!

HOW TO PROPERLY MEASURE INGREDIENTS

It may seem obvious, but I have to stress again that baking is science. You want to make sure that you are always measuring your ingredients carefully and precisely because inaccurate measurements lead to lackluster results. Professional bakers most often use a digital scale to measure ingredients by weight, but I keep things "at-home friendly" by using volume weights in the recipes. (There is a measurement conversion chart in the back of the book if you're feeling like a pro.)

Did you know there is a difference between liquid and dry measuring cups?

- **Dry ingredients:** These call for metal measuring cups that have flat tops (no spout) to make even measurements every time. Try the dip and sweep method: Dip the measuring cup into the package of your ingredient, and use the back of a butter knife or something else with a straight edge to sweep off the excess. You generally don't want to pack ingredients, but there are some that do need to be packed. Brown sugar is the most common of these, so you can use the dip and sweep method, but firmly press the sugar into the cup with your fingers or the back of a spoon. For sticky ingredients like peanut butter, molasses, and corn syrup, spray the measuring cup with nonstick cooking spray before measuring for easy removal.

- **Wet ingredients:** These call for a traditional clear glass or plastic liquid measuring cup with a spout. Set the measuring cup on a flat surface and read from the side at eye level, not from the top, to measure liquids accurately. Some recipes call for more than one wet ingredient to be measured, so make sure to read the recipe beforehand to ensure you work efficiently and guarantee easy cleanup!

HOW TO WORK WITH DOUGH

Kneading Dough: When working with yeasty doughs, you must know the proper technique of kneading, which develops gluten and incorporates air, for it to rise and expand. You can use your electric mixer with a dough hook attached, but kneading with your hands can be therapeutic and a great stress reliever.

Prepare your countertop with flour by dusting (sprinkling lightly with your fingertips), and scrape the dough out of the bowl using a rubber spatula or bowl scraper onto your counter. Keep some extra flour on the side in case the dough is sticky. If so, sprinkle more flour over the top and incorporate it into the dough. Form the dough into a ball. Begin kneading by folding the dough down halfway toward you and pressing outward with the heel of your hands. After every push, turn 45 degrees, until it reaches the desired size. (Rounds and loaves are most common.) Keep kneading until the dough springs back. You don't want to overdo it, as this can add too many air bubbles or develop too much gluten, which will cause the dough to toughen as it bakes.

Proofing Dough: Proofing is the final stage in most bread recipes before baking; it allows the yeast to activate and the bread to expand once more. After kneading your dough to the desired size, place it in a greased bowl or tray. Cover and allow it to rise in a warm place in the kitchen. The proofing time depends on the recipe. The best way to tell if your dough is ready for the oven is to gently touch it; if it bounces back, you're ready to go!

How to Roll Cookie Dough: The dough will likely need to be prepared in advance and chilled before you roll it out. Remove the dough from the refrigerator and let it soften for 10 to 15 minutes. Sprinkle a little bit of flour or place a piece of parchment paper on the countertop. Roll the dough out on the floured surface or parchment paper, using minimal flour to keep the rolling pin from sticking. Roll the dough to ¼- to ½-inch thickness. (I prefer my cookies on the thicker side.) It is important to turn the dough as you roll: Roll the dough once, then give it a quarter turn and roll again. Repeat until you get the desired thickness, adding more flour as you go to keep the dough from sticking.

HOW TO MELT CHOCOLATE AND CANDY MELTS

There are two ways to melt chocolate. First, you can melt it in a double boiler—a heat-safe container, most likely a metal mixing bowl, placed over a saucepan partially filled with boiling water. Place chocolate chips or morsels in the bowl, and let them melt over the steam in the saucepan, stirring constantly with a rubber spatula until fully melted and smooth. Alternatively, you can microwave the chocolate in a heat-safe bowl in 20- to 30-second intervals, stirring in between to ensure even heating. Do not overheat or you will burn the chocolate.

HOW TO GET TO KNOW YOUR OVEN

It is very important for everyone to have a relationship with their oven. Do you really know yours? Here are some questions and suggestions to help build the relationship so that you can have better bakes.

- **Is your oven gas, electric, or convection?** It is important to know how it is powered because you will know where the heat source starts and how it is being produced in your oven. All ovens have a bottom heat source, but gas ovens have a broiling system on the top; electric ovens have electric wires, and convection ovens have a fan that circulates hot air throughout to ensure even baking.

- **How long does it take to preheat your oven?** You should know how long it takes to get to an accurate temperature, as some ovens take quite a bit of time. (Mine takes about 20 minutes to reach 350°F.) An oven thermometer is a great investment to find out what is really going on inside your oven. Don't always believe what the screen says; once you use the thermometer, you will know how much longer you need to wait to preheat or if you need to raise the temperature.

- **How does your oven work?** Learn how your oven works while baking. Do some tests, write some notes, and figure out if you need to make special accommodations, like rotating pans during baking or baking pans one at a time to ensure an even bake. This step truly is a matter of trial and error.

HOW TO ACCOMMODATE FOR ALLERGENS AND DIETARY NEEDS

If you or those you're baking for have or may have food allergies, here are a few handy swaps you can use in all recipes.

Butter = 1:1 swap for coconut oil or dairy-free margarine

Egg = 1 teaspoon xanthan gum or ¼ cup applesauce or ½ smashed banana per egg

Heavy Cream = 1:1 swap for coconut milk (it will add a coconut flavor, so this may not work for all recipes)

Milk = 1:1 swap for soy milk or almond milk

Peanut Butter = 1:1 swap for cream cheese, almond butter, or sunflower seed butter

Peanuts and Tree Nuts = crushed pretzels

HOW TO FROST AND ASSEMBLE A LAYER CAKE

Baking a cake is only half the battle—then you have to make it look delicious! Luckily, I know a thing or two about frosting a cake, and I'm happy to share. First, to truly frost a fabulous cake, you'll need a few specialty items, most of which can be purchased economically at a craft store or online:

- Cake turntable
- Cake board, same diameter as your cake
- Plastic or metal scraper
- Offset spatula
- Decorating bag and tips (optional)

Now you'll just need a little time and patience to devote to creating a work of art. The more often you do it, the less time and patience you'll need. (I promise!)

1. Trim and level the cake's layers with a serrated knife, and soak them with simple syrup—one part water to one part sugar, brought to a boil over medium heat for 3 to 5 minutes, stirred until the sugar is dissolved, and cooled. Use a pastry brush or squeeze bottle to spread evenly.

2. Place a piece of double-sided tape on the bottom of the cake board and attach it to the turntable.

3. Use a spatula to put a dab of frosting directly on the cake board before putting down the first cake layer. This will keep the cake from moving while you frost it.

4. Place the first layer right-side up so that the flat bottom sits on the stand.

5. With a rubber spatula, place a big dollop (about 1 cup) of frosting on top of the first layer. You can also use a decorating bag (no tip) and pipe the icing on top.

6. Using an offset spatula, gently spread the frosting evenly over the top and just past the edge of the top surface. Slowly turn as you spread. The overhang of frosting will help you frost the sides of the cake. Be careful not to damage the cake.

7. Place the second cake layer top-side down so that you have a flat and smooth surface to work with. Gently press down to stick. Take a step back and adjust the cake as needed, making sure it's centered and level. Repeat steps 5 and 6.

8. Start the crumb coat method. A crumb coat is a thin amount of frosting covering the entire cake to seal the crumbs and create a smooth finish. Add a thin layer of buttercream to the top of the cake and then the sides, using an offset spatula. Scrape any buttercream with crumbs into another bowl. Chill the cake in the refrigerator for 20 to 30 minutes.

9. When the cake is cold, add a final coat of frosting by spreading a generous amount of buttercream on the top and sides. An alternative way is to pipe icing all over the cake and then spread.

10. Gently smooth the sides with a cake scraper while turning the turntable. Pull the excess buttercream on the top edge of the cake toward the center of the cake with the offset spatula. The finished, iced cake should have a level top with straight, even sides. You can also leave it textured or swirled with an offset spatula, if desired.

11. Add borders, writing, flowers, or any other decorations.

HOW TO FILL AND PIPE WITH A DECORATING BAG

1. Insert a coupler base into your pastry bag, then snip off the tip, making a hole just large enough to accommodate the coupler.

2. Fit the bag with your tip and secure it with the coupler ring.

3. Place the bag, tip down, in a drinking glass, and fold the ends around the rim so that it stands up.

4. Scoop icing into the open bag with a rubber or offset spatula. Do not fill more than ⅔ full. Once filled, pinch and squeeze the wide end of the bag until all the icing flows to the tip. Twist the bag where the filling starts to close the bag and prevent spillage when piping.

5. To pipe, hold the bag with your dominant hand where the bag is twisted, Squeeze the bag with your palm, as you can control pressure when squeezing. Use your opposite hand to help direct and hold the bag as you pipe.

BASIC DECORATING TIPS

- **Basket Weave Tips:** Used for piping smooth or textured ribbons.

- **Leaf Tips:** Used for piping—you guessed it—leaves. You can also pipe borders and scallops.

- **Rose Tips:** Used for making flower petals, roses, scallops, and ruffles; these tips have a slit-shaped opening with one end wider than the other.

- **Round Tips:** Used for piping dots, lines, beads, vines, little flowers, and lettering.

- **Star Tips:** Used for piping borders, stars, rosettes, and shells.

ABOUT THE RECIPES

The recipes in this book are meant to be fun! Some are super simple, while others require a bit more time and skill, but all are worth it in the end. One of my favorite things about baking is that even if a bake isn't perfect, it's probably still delicious. Remember to check my list of swaps on page 11 if you have a food allergy or are baking for those who do. Many recipes contain tips for swapping ingredients and troubleshooting techniques, and even though you've learned how to frost like a pro, the multi-layer cake recipes include instructions on how to frost your cakes directly on a cake plate or platter. Finally, follow my list of "Sweet Rules" and you can't go wrong:

- **Read through every recipe all the way before starting.** Take notes and plan out everything you need—including your time—before starting to avoid any confusion.

- **Mise en place is important.** This means having your ingredients, bakeware, and kitchen prepared before you start baking. If you practice this rule, you will be very efficient and organized.

- **Preheat your oven.** The most crucial rule! So important, in fact, that it's the first step of nearly every recipe. All ovens perform differently, so learn yours, as I described in the previous section, and *preheat*.

☙ **Use top-quality and fresh ingredients.** Be sure that your ingredients are of high quality and prepared as the recipe states. For example, if your recipe says the butter must be melted, be sure it is melted before advancing.

☙ **Take pictures of your finished work and show it off!** You earned it. Be proud of your unique creations.

☙ **Last but not least, have fun!** Baking is meant to be enjoyed and shared, so keep a smile on your face and share your bakes with those you love.

Chapter 2
SPRING RECIPES

Cinnamon Swirl King Cake

✢ SERVES 10 ✤

PREP TIME: **15 MINUTES** • COOK TIME: **1 HOUR**

. . . .

*B*ourbon Street, Mardi Gras, throwing those beads—I love all that stuff. And my friend Kisha, a New Orleans native, taught me that to properly celebrate Mardi Gras, you've got to have a king cake, so this one's for her. A traditional king cake is a colorful, labor-intensive, vanilla-and-cinnamon-flavored pastry ring with a surprise inside. My king cake recipe has all the flavors and pageantry of the original but is quick and easy to make. It's a vanilla cake with a cinnamon-pecan swirl, topped with the classic purple, gold, and green glitter, and don't forget that plastic baby hidden inside! The lucky person who finds it gets a year of prosperity *and* hosts next year's Mardi Gras party.

. . . .

FOR THE CAKE

Butter and flour or cooking spray, for preparing the pan

2½ cups all-purpose flour

1 teaspoon baking powder

½ teaspoon baking soda

½ teaspoon kosher salt

1 cup granulated sugar

¾ cup (1½ sticks) unsalted butter, at room temperature

¾ cup milk

3 large eggs

1 tablespoon vanilla extract

FOR THE FILLING

1 cup toasted pecan pieces, finely chopped

¾ cup light brown sugar

2 teaspoons ground cinnamon

FOR DECORATING

1 cup confectioners' sugar

2 to 4 tablespoons milk

Purple sanding sugar

Green sanding sugar

Gold sanding sugar

. . . .

1. **To make the cake,** preheat the oven to 350°F and prepare a Bundt pan by greasing it with butter and dusting it with flour or coating it with cooking spray.

2. In a medium bowl, stir together the flour, baking powder, baking soda, and salt.

3. In a large bowl using an electric mixer or in the bowl of a stand mixer, cream together the sugar and butter on medium speed until pale yellow and fluffy. Add the milk, eggs, and vanilla and beat on medium speed until well incorporated. Add the dry ingredients in two or three batches, beating in between until just incorporated.

4. **To make the filling,** in a separate medium bowl, stir together the pecans, brown sugar, and cinnamon.
5. Pour one-third of the batter into the prepared Bundt pan and then sprinkle half of the filling mixture over the batter. Add half of the remaining batter in an even layer and then all the remaining filling. Pour the remaining batter on top.
6. Bake for 55 to 60 minutes, or until the cake is golden brown on top and firm to the touch. Remove the pan from the oven and set it on a wire rack to cool for about 10 minutes.
7. If you're using a plastic baby, insert it into the bottom of the cake before removing the cake from the pan.
8. Once the cake has cooled for 10 minutes or so, invert it onto a platter. Let cool completely before decorating.
9. **To make the decorations,** in a small bowl, whisk together the confectioners' sugar and 2 tablespoons of milk until smooth. Add additional milk a little at a time to achieve the right consistency for drizzling.
10. Once the cake has cooled completely, drizzle the glaze generously over the top, letting it run down the sides. Sprinkle the purple, green, and gold sanding sugars on top in alternating sections or stripes.

TECHNIQUE TIP: To toast the pecans, spread the pieces in a single layer on a baking sheet and bake for about 6 to 8 minutes in a 350°F oven.

Bouquet of Cupcakes

⇒ MAKES 12 CUPCAKES ⇐

PREP TIME: **30 MINUTES** • COOK TIME: **20 MINUTES**

. . . .

*O*nce, when my little sisters Khaliyah and Khylee were babies, they helped me make cupcakes for Easter that we decorated like pretty flowers. We've kept up the tradition of getting together to bake and decorate fun desserts for holidays ever since. This array of flower cupcakes arranged into a bouquet is the perfect way to show Mom how much you care on Mother's Day.

. . . .

FOR THE CUPCAKES

1½ cups all-purpose flour

1½ teaspoons
baking powder

¼ teaspoon kosher salt

½ cup (1 stick) unsalted
butter, at room temperature

1 cup granulated sugar

2 large eggs

2 teaspoons vanilla extract

½ cup milk

FOR THE FROSTING

¾ cup unsalted butter, at
room temperature

2½ to 3¼ cups
confectioners' sugar

3 tablespoons milk

¼ teaspoon kosher salt

1 teaspoon vanilla extract

FOR DECORATING

Pink gel food coloring

Lavender gel food coloring

Green gel food coloring

Mint leaves, for garnish

. . . .

1. **To make the cupcakes,** preheat the oven to 350°F and line a 12-cup muffin tin with paper cupcake liners.
2. In a medium bowl, combine the flour, baking powder, and salt.
3. In a large bowl using an electric mixer or in the bowl of a stand mixer, cream together the butter and sugar on high speed until pale yellow and fluffy. Add the eggs one at a time, beating until incorporated. Add the vanilla and beat until incorporated. Add half of the flour mixture and beat on medium speed until incorporated. Scrape down the sides of the bowl, add

the milk, and beat until incorporated. Scrape down the bowl again and add the remaining flour mixture. Beat just until incorporated.

4. Scoop the batter into the prepared muffin tin, filling each cup about two-thirds full. Bake for 18 to 20 minutes, until a toothpick inserted in the center comes out clean. Let the cupcakes cool in the pan for a minute or two, then transfer to a rack to cool completely.

5. **To make the frosting,** in a medium bowl using an electric mixer or in the bowl of a stand mixer, beat the butter on medium-high speed until

creamy. Add 2½ cups of confectioners' sugar along with the milk, salt, and vanilla. Beat together until well combined. Add additional confectioners' sugar as needed to achieve the desired consistency.

6. Put half the frosting in one bowl and add a few drops of pink gel food coloring. Put two-thirds of the remaining frosting in a separate bowl and add a couple of drops of lavender gel food coloring. Add 1 or 2 drops of green gel food coloring to the remaining frosting.

7. **To decorate the cupcakes,** fit a piping bag with a drop flower piping tip. Add the pink and lavender frosting to the piping bag in large, alternating spoonfuls. Fill the bag about two-thirds full.

8. Pipe stars onto half of the cupcakes by placing the tip close to the surface of the cupcake, squeezing out a bit of frosting, and then lifting the bag straight up. Cover the entire surface of the cupcake with frosting stars.

9. For the other half of the cupcakes, fit a piping bag with a closed star tip and fill the bag two-thirds full of pink frosting. Start in the middle of the cupcake, holding the tip just above the surface, and use medium pressure to pipe the frosting into a tight spiral from the center all the way out to the edge of the cupcake. When you get toward the end, reduce the pressure on the bag and let the frosting trail off. Repeat the same process on each cupcake, making a second layer of frosting.

10. **To assemble the bouquet,** arrange the cupcakes, alternating between the different frosting designs, in a circular shape on a large, oval platter or a baking sheet. Tuck the mint leaves in and around the cupcakes.

11. Fit a piping bag with an open star tip and fill it with the green frosting. Pipe several stems coming down from the flowers and coming together in a bunch.

12. Use the pink or pink-and-lavender frosting to pipe a bow on top of the stems.

ADVANCED TIP: If you want to make your bouquet even prettier, get edible flowers or flower petals (these can be purchased from your local cake supply store, but make sure they are organic and meant for eating to ensure that they don't have harmful chemicals on them) and add them to the arrangement.

Pasta and Meatballs Cake

⚜ SERVES 10 ⚜

PREP TIME: 1 HOUR 15 MINUTES • COOK TIME: 35 MINUTES

. . . .

I love April Fools' Day pranks, as long as they are in good fun—and that means no hurt feelings. So what better way to pull a fast one on April 1 than to serve a pile of delicious pasta—my favorite food in the world—that turns out to be a sweet, moist chocolate cake? No one could be mad about that.

. . . .

FOR THE CAKE LAYERS

Butter or nonstick cooking spray, for greasing the pans

3 cups all-purpose flour

3 cups granulated sugar

1½ cups unsweetened cocoa powder

1 tablespoon baking soda

1½ teaspoons baking powder

1 teaspoon kosher salt

4 large eggs

1½ cups buttermilk

1½ cups brewed coffee, warm

½ cup vegetable oil

1 tablespoon vanilla extract

FOR THE FROSTING

1 cup (2 sticks) unsalted butter, at room temperature

4 to 5 cups confectioners' sugar

¼ cup milk

¼ teaspoon kosher salt

2 teaspoons vanilla extract

FOR DECORATING

Yellow gel food coloring

½ teaspoon cocoa powder

¾ cup strawberry preserves, warmed slightly in the microwave to make it a bit runny

2 ounces white chocolate

. . . .

1. **To make the cake,** preheat the oven to 350°F. Lightly grease 3 (8-inch) round cake pans with cooking spray or butter, and line the pans with parchment paper.

2. In a medium bowl, whisk together the flour, sugar, cocoa, baking soda, baking powder, and salt.

3. In a large bowl using an electric mixer or in the bowl of a stand mixer, beat the eggs, buttermilk, coffee, oil, and vanilla on medium speed for about 2 minutes,

until smooth. Add the flour mixture and beat just until well incorporated. Do not overmix.

4. Divide the batter evenly among the prepared cake pans. Bake for about 35 minutes, until the top springs back when pressed and a toothpick inserted in the center comes out clean.

5. Remove the pans from the oven and let the cakes cool in the pans for about 10 minutes before inverting them onto a wire rack to cool completely.

6. **To make the frosting,** in a medium bowl using an electric mixer or in the bowl of a stand mixer, beat the butter until creamy. Add 4 cups of confectioners' sugar, the milk, the salt, and the vanilla and beat together until well combined. Add additional confectioners' sugar as needed to achieve the desired consistency.

7. **To assemble and decorate the cake,** use a serrated knife to level the tops of two of the cake layers. (Reserve the third cake layer for decorating.)

8. Place the first layer, cut-side down, on your cake plate and top it with a layer of frosting. Repeat with the second layer.

9. Spread frosting in an even layer over the sides of the cake.

10. Add a few drops of yellow gel food coloring and the cocoa to the remaining frosting to tint—it should be pasta-colored.

11. Transfer the frosting to a piping bag fitted with a small round tip or to a resealable plastic bag with a small hole snipped in one of the corners. Pipe the frosting all over the top of the cake, swirling and looping it around so that it looks like a pile of spaghetti. The spaghetti should be piled all over the top of the cake and hang over the edges.

12. **To make the meatballs,** in a medium bowl, crumble the remaining cake layer into crumbs. Using your hands, scoop up some of the crumbs and press them into a meatball-size ball, about 1½ inches. Once you have a nice, firm ball, roll it in the crumbs to coat. If the crumbs don't want to stick, spritz the cake balls with a little water before rolling in the crumbs. Repeat until you have 7 to 9 meatballs.

13. Spoon some of the preserves onto the cake to make a puddle of sauce. Arrange the meatballs on top and then spoon more sauce over each of the meatballs.

14. Using a zester, grate the white chocolate over the top to look like freshly grated Parmesan cheese.

SUBSTITUTION TIP: Instead of making the meatballs out of the extra layer of cake, you could make this as a three-layer cake and use chocolate-hazelnut candies, like Ferrero Rocher, as the meatballs.

Springy Chocolate Bark

My family loves chocolate bark, and they request it for every holiday, especially during spring. With all the pretty pastel-colored candies appearing around this time of year, it's fun to add a sweet and seasonal spin on candy bark. Use a layer of white chocolate to keep the color palette seasonally appropriate, pick up your favorite candies, and you can't go wrong!

8 ounces semisweet chocolate, chopped

8 ounces white chocolate, chopped

½ cup Robin Eggs candies, some crushed

½ cup pastel-colored M&Ms, some crushed

¼ cup pastel sprinkles

1. Line a large, rimmed baking sheet with parchment paper.
2. Place the semisweet chocolate in a microwave-safe bowl and heat in 30-second intervals, stirring in between, until the chocolate is completely melted and smooth.
3. Pour the chocolate onto the prepared baking sheet and spread it out in an even layer. Chill in the refrigerator until it is set, 15 to 20 minutes.
4. Place the white chocolate in a microwave-safe bowl and melt the same way you did the semisweet chocolate. Once it is fully melted and smooth, let it cool for 5 to 10 minutes, then pour it over the chilled semisweet chocolate. Spread it out in an even layer and immediately scatter the Robin Eggs, M&Ms, and sprinkles over the top, pressing them in a bit.
5. Chill in the refrigerator for about 20 minutes more. Break into pieces and serve at room temperature.

SUBSTITUTION TIP: If you're not a fan of white chocolate, you can substitute milk chocolate for the top layer.

Springtime Confetti Bars

✦ MAKES 8 BARS ✦

PREP TIME: **15 MINUTES** • COOK TIME: **25 MINUTES**

. . . .

*N*ow, I'm not one to throw shade at Punxsutawney Phil the groundhog, but these pretty dessert bars will do a much better job of telling you when spring is coming. They're ooey-gooey, finger-licking delicious—the perfect way to celebrate the coming of spring. I like to use pastel-colored sprinkles for these, both inside the cookie bars and on top. They're great for Easter, Mother's Day, or a springtime garden party!

. . . .

FOR THE BARS

Nonstick cooking spray, for greasing the pan

¾ cup granulated sugar

½ cup unsalted butter, at room temperature

1 large egg

2 teaspoons vanilla extract

1½ cups all-purpose flour

¼ teaspoon kosher salt

1 teaspoon baking powder

½ teaspoon baking soda

1½ teaspoons cornstarch

½ cup pastel-colored sprinkles

FOR THE FROSTING AND DECORATIONS

6 tablespoons unsalted butter, at room temperature

½ cup plus 2 tablespoons confectioners' sugar

1½ tablespoons milk

½ teaspoon vanilla extract

Pinch kosher salt

Gel food coloring (optional)

Pastel-colored sprinkles

. . . .

1. **To make the bars,** preheat the oven to 350°F and coat an 8-inch square baking pan with nonstick cooking spray.

2. In a large bowl using an electric mixer or in the bowl of a stand mixer, cream together the sugar and butter on medium-high speed until pale yellow and fluffy. Add the egg and vanilla and beat to incorporate.

3. In a separate bowl, stir together the flour, salt, baking powder, baking soda, and cornstarch.

4. With the mixer on low speed, add the dry ingredients to the wet ingredients in three batches, beating until fully combined.

5. Add the sprinkles and beat on low speed until incorporated.

CONTINUED >>

6. Press the cookie dough into the prepared pan with your hands, patting it into an even layer. Bake until the top is lightly browned, about 25 minutes.

7. Remove the pan from the oven, set it on a wire rack, and let it cool completely.

8. **To make the frosting,** in a medium bowl using an electric mixer or in the bowl of a stand mixer, beat the butter for about 2 minutes on medium speed, until smooth and creamy.

9. With the mixer running on low speed, add the confectioners' sugar, milk, vanilla, and salt. Raise the speed to high and beat for 3 more minutes. Add a drop of food coloring (if using) and beat to incorporate.

10. Spread the frosting evenly over the cooled cookie bars and scatter the sprinkles on top. Using a sharp knife, cut into squares.

TECHNIQUE TIP: To make it easy to remove the cookie bars from the pan, make a sling out of foil or parchment paper by lining the bottom of the pan and leaving extra overhanging two sides. You can use this sling to lift the cookie bars out of the pan before frosting and cutting.

Cinnamon Sugar Churro Cupcakes

↯ MAKES 16 CUPCAKES ↯

PREP TIME: **45 MINUTES** • COOK TIME: **20 MINUTES**

*T*he first time I had churros was at a rodeo in my home state of Texas. If you haven't had them before, all you need to know is that they are deep-fried dough heavily coated with cinnamon sugar. I loved them so much that I wanted to capture that cinnamon-sugar flavor in a cupcake to serve on Cinco de Mayo. These moist, cinnamon-scented vanilla cupcakes are topped with a cinnamon-flavored cream cheese frosting and finished with cinnamon sanding sugar.

FOR THE CUPCAKES

1⅔ cups all-purpose flour

1 cup granulated sugar

1½ teaspoons baking powder

½ teaspoon baking soda

1 teaspoon ground cinnamon

¼ teaspoon kosher salt

¾ cup (1½ sticks) unsalted butter, at room temperature

3 large egg whites, at room temperature

½ cup sour cream, at room temperature

½ cup milk, at room temperature

1 tablespoon vanilla extract

FOR THE FROSTING

4 ounces cream cheese, at room temperature

½ cup (1 stick) unsalted butter, at room temperature

4 cups confectioners' sugar

½ teaspoon ground cinnamon

¼ teaspoon kosher salt

2 teaspoons vanilla extract

2 to 4 tablespoons milk

FOR FINISHING

⅓ cup sanding sugar

2 tablespoons ground cinnamon

1. **To make the cupcakes,** preheat the oven to 350°F and line a 12-cup muffin tin with paper cupcake liners.
2. In a medium bowl, whisk together the flour, sugar, baking powder, baking soda, cinnamon, and salt.
3. In a large bowl using an electric mixer or in the bowl of a stand mixer, beat the butter on medium speed until fluffy. Add the egg whites and beat to combine. Add the sour cream, milk, and vanilla and beat until well incorporated.
4. Add the dry ingredients to the wet ingredients in two or three batches, beating in between additions to incorporate.

5. Scoop the batter into the prepared muffin tin, dividing evenly and filling each cup about three-fourths full. Bake until the tops are golden brown and spring back when pressed, 18 to 20 minutes.

6. Remove the pan from the oven and let the cupcakes cool for several minutes before transferring them to a wire rack. Let cool completely before frosting.

7. **To make the frosting,** in a large bowl using an electric mixer or in the bowl of a stand mixer, beat together the cream cheese and butter until fluffy and well combined. Add 1 cup of confectioners' sugar, the cinnamon, and the salt and beat to combine. Add the remaining 3 cups of confectioners' sugar in three batches, beating after each addition to incorporate. Add the vanilla and beat to incorporate.

8. Add the milk one tablespoon at a time, beating on medium speed until the mixture reaches the desired consistency. (You may not need to use all of the milk.)

9. Once the cupcakes are completely cooled, pipe the frosting on top.

10. In a small bowl, stir together the sanding sugar and cinnamon and sprinkle the mixture generously over the frosted cupcakes.

Meyer Lemon Pound Cake

⚘ SERVES 10 ⚘
PREP TIME: **15 MINUTES** • COOK TIME: **1 HOUR**

. . . .

*T*he bright tartness and pretty yellow color of Meyer lemons make this cake a great fit for springtime celebrations. Like any pound cake, it is dense, rich, and moist—a lovely dessert for a garden party, brunch, or lunch.

. . . .

FOR THE CAKE

Nonstick cooking spray, for greasing the pan

1½ cups all-purpose flour

½ teaspoon baking powder

½ teaspoon kosher salt

¾ cup (1½ sticks) unsalted butter, at room temperature

1 cup granulated sugar

3 large eggs, at room temperature

¼ cup sour cream, at room temperature

Zest and juice of 1 Meyer lemon

1 teaspoon vanilla extract

FOR THE GLAZE

1 cup confectioners' sugar, sifted

1½ tablespoons Meyer lemon juice

1 tablespoon milk

. . . .

1. **To make the cake,** preheat the oven to 350°F and coat a 9-by-5-inch loaf pan with nonstick cooking spray.
2. In a large bowl, whisk together the flour, baking powder, and salt.
3. In a separate large bowl using an electric mixer or in the bowl of a stand mixer, cream together the butter and sugar on medium-high speed until pale yellow and fluffy, about 3 minutes.
4. Set the mixer to low speed and, with the mixer running, add the eggs one at a time, beating to incorporate after each addition. Add the sour cream, lemon zest and juice, and vanilla and beat on medium speed to incorporate.
5. Add the dry ingredients to the wet ingredients in several batches, beating after each to incorporate. After the last addition, beat on high speed until the mixture is smooth, about 15 seconds more.
6. Transfer the batter to the prepared pan. Bake until a toothpick inserted into the

center comes out mostly clean, 45 to 60 minutes.

7. Set the cake on a wire rack and let cool in the pan for about an hour before removing it.

8. **To make the glaze,** in a small bowl, stir together the confectioners' sugar, lemon juice, and milk. Pour the glaze over the cake when it is still a bit warm. Serve at room temperature.

SUBSTITUTION TIP: If you don't have Meyer lemons, you can substitute regular lemons.

Luck o' the Irish Cupcakes

⤙ MAKES 12 CUPCAKES ⤚

PREP TIME: **30 MINUTES** • COOK TIME: **20 MINUTES**

I am not one bit Irish, but I sure am lucky! The definition of "luck of the Irish" is "extreme good fortune," and I assure you that's how you'll feel if you make these cupcakes. They start with moist chocolate cake and are topped with Irish cream buttercream frosting, rainbows, and, of course, a pot of gold. Let's make this recipe together, and I will meet you at the end of the rainbow.

FOR THE CUPCAKES

1 cup all-purpose flour

¾ cup unsweetened cocoa powder

1 teaspoon baking powder

¼ teaspoon kosher salt

½ cup (1 stick) unsalted butter, at room temperature

1 cup granulated sugar

2 large eggs

¼ cup strong brewed coffee, at room temperature

¼ cup plus 1 tablespoon Irish cream liqueur

FOR THE FROSTING

½ cup (1 stick) unsalted butter, at room temperature

2 to 2½ cups confectioners' sugar

1 tablespoon Irish cream liqueur

Green gel food coloring

FOR DECORATING

12 mini peanut butter cups

Gold sanding sugar

6 strips rainbow stripe candy (like Airheads Extreme), cut in half

1. **To make the cupcakes,** preheat the oven to 350°F and line a 12-cup muffin tin with paper cupcake liners.

2. In a medium bowl, whisk together the flour, cocoa, baking powder, and salt.

3. In a large bowl using an electric mixer or in the bowl of a stand mixer, cream together the butter and sugar on medium speed until fluffy. Add the eggs one at a time, beating after each to incorporate. Add the coffee and Irish cream liqueur and beat until well incorporated.

4. Add the dry ingredients to the wet ingredients in two or three batches, beating in between additions to incorporate.

5. Scoop the batter into the prepared muffin tin, dividing evenly and filling each cup about three-fourths full. Bake until the tops spring back when pressed, 18 to 20 minutes.

6. Remove the pan from the oven and let the cupcakes cool for several minutes before transferring them to a wire rack. Let cool completely before frosting.

7. **To make the frosting,** beat the butter on medium speed until smooth. Add 2 cups of confectioners' sugar about ½ cup at a time, and beat until smooth, then add additional confectioners' sugar a couple of tablespoons at a time until you reach the desired consistency. Finally, add the Irish cream liqueur and 2 to 3 drops of food coloring and beat to incorporate.

8. Once the cupcakes are completely cooled, transfer the frosting to a piping bag fitted with a round or open star tip or to a resealable plastic bag with a corner snipped off to make a piping bag. Pipe the frosting on top of the cupcakes.

9. **To decorate,** unwrap the peanut butter cups and pipe a small dollop of frosting on top of each. Put the gold sanding sugar in a small dish and press the frosted top of each peanut butter cup into it so that the sugar covers the whole top of the peanut butter cup. Set one "pot of gold" on top of the frosting on each cupcake, placing it a bit off to one side. Next, form one piece of rainbow stripe candy into an arch. Set one side of the arch into the frosting and the other into the "pot of gold." Repeat with the remaining cupcakes.

Margarita Cookies with Lime Glaze

✦ MAKES ABOUT 4 DOZEN COOKIES ✦

PREP TIME: 20 MINUTES, PLUS 1 HOUR TO CHILL • COOK TIME: 15 MINUTES

When I turned 21, all I wanted was a margarita—my favorite cocktail—so of course I had to try turning those flavors into a cookie. These crunchy treats are flavored with lime and orange zest plus a shot of tequila. A tart lime glaze and a salty-sweet coating finish them off.

FOR THE COOKIES

1 cup (2 sticks) unsalted butter, at room temperature

1 cup granulated sugar

1 large egg, at room temperature

1 tablespoon tequila

1 tablespoon grated lime zest (from about 2 limes)

1 teaspoon grated orange zest (from about ½ orange)

2 cups all-purpose flour

¼ teaspoon kosher salt

FOR THE SUGAR COATING

½ cup sanding sugar

½ teaspoon kosher salt

FOR THE GLAZE

1 cup confectioners' sugar

2 tablespoons freshly squeezed lime juice

1 teaspoon grated lime zest

1. **To make the cookies,** in a large bowl using an electric mixer or in the bowl of a stand mixer, cream together the butter and sugar on medium-high speed until pale yellow and fluffy.

2. Add the egg, tequila, lime zest, and orange zest and beat on medium speed to incorporate.

3. Add the flour and salt and beat on low just until fully incorporated.

4. Divide the dough into two equal pieces and roll each into a log about 6 inches long and about 1½ to 2 inches in diameter. Wrap each log in plastic wrap and refrigerate for 1 hour.

5. Preheat the oven to 350°F and stir together the sanding sugar and salt to make the sugar coating.

6. Spread the sanding sugar mixture in a thin layer on your work surface, unwrap the logs of dough, and roll each log in the sugar to coat well.

7. Cut the logs into ¼-inch-thick rounds and arrange them on a baking sheet. Bake until the cookies are lightly browned, about 15 minutes.

CONTINUED >>

8. Remove the pan from the oven and let the cookies cool for a minute or two before transferring them to a wire rack to cool completely.

9. **To make the lime glaze,** in a small bowl, stir together the confectioners' sugar and lime juice until smooth.

10. Once the cookies are completely cooled, drizzle the glaze over the top along with the lime zest. Serve at room temperature.

TROUBLESHOOTING TIP: If the dough logs are difficult to slice, they may not be cold enough. Chill them in the freezer for about 20 minutes and use a serrated knife to cut them.

Chocolate Hazelnut Bread Pudding

❖ SERVES 10 ❖

PREP TIME: 15 MINUTES, PLUS 15 MINUTES STANDING TIME • COOK TIME: 40 MINUTES

*T*his dessert reminds me of the Nutella sandwiches my mom used to make me when I was a kid. I created something similar while I was in culinary school because I wanted to capture those nostalgic flavors in a more elevated dessert. This bread pudding is simple to make and always gets rave reviews.

Butter or nonstick cooking spray, for greasing the pan

1 loaf challah or brioche bread, preferably a day or two old, sliced

1¼ cups chocolate-hazelnut spread

2 large eggs

½ cup granulated sugar

1¼ cups heavy (whipping) cream

1 teaspoon vanilla extract

Pinch kosher salt

1. Preheat the oven to 350°F and coat a 2-quart baking dish with butter or cooking spray.
2. Make sandwiches with the challah or brioche and chocolate-hazelnut spread and then cut the sandwiches into 2-inch squares. Place the sandwich pieces in the prepared baking dish.
3. In a large bowl, whisk together the eggs and sugar. Whisk in the cream, vanilla, and salt.
4. Pour the egg mixture over the sandwich pieces and let stand for 15 minutes to allow the bread to absorb the mixture.
5. Cover the baking dish with aluminum foil and bake for 30 minutes. Remove the foil from the baking dish and bake for 10 minutes more. Serve warm.

SUBSTITUTION TIP: Instead of sliced brioche or challah bread, use 5 croissants, each split in half.

Easter Bunny Carrot Cupcakes

⸙ MAKES 12 CUPCAKES ⸙

PREP TIME: **30 MINUTES** • COOK TIME: **20 MINUTES**

. . . .

I was first asked to create Easter bunny cupcakes when I was working in a bakery. Rather than focusing on the ears, nose, and whiskers, I thought I'd be a bit cheeky and make them tushy-side up. This is that recipe—these bunny butts are so adorable!

. . . .

FOR THE CUPCAKES

1⅔ cups all-purpose flour

1½ teaspoons ground cinnamon

1 teaspoon baking soda

½ teaspoon baking powder

1 teaspoon kosher salt

¼ teaspoon ground nutmeg

¼ teaspoon ground cloves

¾ cup neutral-flavored oil

½ cup granulated sugar

½ cup brown sugar

3 large eggs

2 teaspoons vanilla extract

2 carrots, grated

FOR THE FROSTING

1 (8-ounce) package cream cheese, at room temperature

½ cup (1 stick) unsalted butter, at room temperature

1 teaspoon vanilla extract

3 to 4 cups confectioners' sugar

Green gel food coloring

FOR DECORATING

4 ounces white fondant

Pink food marker

Sanding sugar

. . . .

1. **To make the cupcakes,** preheat the oven to 350°F and line a 12-cup muffin tin with paper cupcake liners.

2. In a medium bowl, whisk together the flour, cinnamon, baking soda, baking powder, salt, nutmeg, and cloves.

3. In a large bowl using an electric mixer or in the bowl of a stand mixer, combine the oil with both sugars and stir until the mixture is smooth. Add the eggs one at a time, beating after each to incorporate. Add the vanilla and mix to incorporate.

4. Add the dry ingredients to the wet ingredients in several batches, mixing to incorporate after each addition. Gently fold in the carrots.

5. Scoop the batter into the prepared muffin tin, filling each cup about three-fourths full. Bake for 18 to 20 minutes, until a toothpick inserted in the center of one of the cupcakes comes out clean.

6. Remove the pan from the oven and set it on a wire rack. Let the cupcakes cool completely.

7. **Meanwhile, make the frosting.** In a medium bowl using an electric mixer or in the bowl of a stand mixer, cream together the cream cheese, butter, and vanilla on medium-high speed until smooth. Add 3 cups of confectioners' sugar; then add the remaining 1 cup a little at a time, beating until it is fully incorporated and the right consistency.

8. Transfer half of the frosting to a separate bowl and stir in 3 to 4 drops of green food coloring. (The other half of the frosting will stay white.)

9. **To make the bunnies' feet,** roll out the fondant into a thin sheet. Use a small oval or drop-shaped cutter or a sharp paring knife to cut out 24 "feet."

10. Use the food marker to draw pink pads onto the feet—three for toes and a larger one for the heel.

11. Once the cupcakes are completely cooled, use a small spatula or a butter knife to spread a layer of green frosting over the top of each cupcake.

Put the remaining green frosting into a piping bag fitted with a grass tip (a tip with several small holes in it, like the Wilton #233). Pipe a ring of "grass" around the outside edge of the cupcake by holding the tip just above the cake, squeezing, and then lifting straight up. This may take some practice, but you can always scrape off the frosting and begin again.

12. Use a small cookie scoop to scoop white frosting onto the top of the cupcakes (inside the ring of grass) to serve as the bunny's body (or, more specifically, the bunny's tushy).

13. Take a small dollop of frosting (the size of a large blueberry) and roll it in the sanding sugar. Place this on top of the bunny's tushy to serve as the tail.

14. Arrange the feet, two per cupcake, so that they are leaning against the bunny's tushy sticking up out of the grass.

15. Serve immediately.

SUBSTITUTION TIP: Instead of piping green frosting for the grass, you can toss 1 cup of sweetened, shredded coconut with a few drops of green food coloring until it is well coated. After spreading frosting on top of the cupcakes, press each cupcake into the coconut to coat it well. This will create the look of grass.

Banana Nut Bread

✣ SERVES 10 ✦

PREP TIME: **15 MINUTES** • COOK TIME: **1 HOUR**

. . . .

My mother, Casika, and stepfather, Kevin, have friends who always give them fruit, and they can never eat all the bananas. Instead of wasting them, the bananas are given to me; I turn them into this Banana Nut Bread and deliver it back to them. It's a perfect solution—their bananas don't go to waste, and they get to enjoy this delicious quick bread on the regular.

. . . .

Nonstick cooking spray, for greasing the pan

2 cups all-purpose flour

1 teaspoon baking soda

¼ teaspoon kosher salt

½ teaspoon ground cinnamon

½ cup (1 stick) unsalted butter, at room temperature

¾ cup brown sugar

2 large eggs, at room temperature

⅓ cup sour cream

4 large, very ripe bananas, mashed

1 teaspoon vanilla extract

¾ cup chopped walnuts

. . . .

1. Preheat the oven to 350°F and coat a 9-by-5-inch loaf pan with nonstick cooking spray.

2. In a large bowl, whisk together the flour, baking soda, salt, and cinnamon.

3. In a separate large bowl using an electric mixer or in the bowl of a stand mixer, cream together the butter and brown sugar on high speed until smooth, about 2 minutes.

4. Reduce the mixer speed to medium and add the eggs one at a time, beating after each addition to incorporate. Add the sour cream, bananas, and vanilla and continue to beat until well combined.

5. Reduce the mixer speed to low and add the dry ingredients in several batches, beating after each until fully incorporated. With a rubber spatula, gently fold in the nuts.

6. Transfer the batter to the prepared loaf pan. Bake for 30 minutes, then cover the pan with aluminum foil and continue to bake for about 30 minutes more, until a toothpick inserted in the center comes out clean.

7. Remove the pan from the oven, set it on a wire rack, and let the bread cool completely. Serve at room temperature.

SUBSTITUTION TIP: You can substitute whole-milk yogurt for the sour cream if you like. And if you only have salted butter, just use what you have and leave out the ¼ teaspoon of salt.

Strawberry Lemon Pancakes

✣ MAKES ABOUT 12 PANCAKES ✣

PREP TIME: 15 MINUTES • COOK TIME: 20 MINUTES

. . . .

*E*veryone should have a good breakfast to kick off the day and set the mood. Sweet strawberries and tart lemon make these pancakes bright, cheery, and fun. Customize them however you like, such as by drizzling them with maple or fruit-based syrup, sprinkling confectioners' sugar on top, or piling on fruit, nuts, yogurt, or whipped cream.

. . . .

1½ cups flour

1 tablespoon granulated sugar

1 tablespoon baking powder

¼ teaspoon kosher salt

2 tablespoons vegetable oil

1 large egg

1¼ cups milk

Zest of 1 lemon

2 tablespoons freshly squeezed lemon juice

Butter, for cooking and serving

¾ cup sliced strawberries

Maple syrup or confectioners' sugar, for serving (optional)

. . . .

1. In a large bowl, whisk together the flour, sugar, baking powder, and salt. Add the oil, egg, milk, lemon zest, and lemon juice and stir to mix.

2. In a medium skillet over medium-high heat, melt about 1 tablespoon of butter. Pour about ¼ cup of batter into the skillet for each pancake and immediately drop several strawberry slices onto each pancake. Cook until the bubbles on the top don't fill in immediately when they pop, 2 to 3 minutes. Gently flip each pancake over and cook on the second side for about 2 minutes more, until browned.

3. Serve the pancakes warm, topped with butter and maple syrup or confectioners' sugar (if using).

SUBSTITUTION TIP: Strawberries are abundant in the springtime, but feel free to substitute other fruits throughout the year. Blackberries, blueberries, or peaches are delicious in the summer, or try pears in the fall or winter.

White Chocolate Raspberry Cheesecake

❖ SERVES 10 ❖

PREP TIME: 30 MINUTES, PLUS 5 HOURS 15 MINUTES TO COOL AND CHILL

COOK TIME: 1 HOUR 30 MINUTES

. . . .

*T*his cake is an accidental trash-into-treasure story! Now, I'm not pointing fingers, but someone overbaked some cookies at the bakery where I used to work. They couldn't be sold, but I didn't want them to go to waste. I tossed them into the food processor with some melted butter and turned them into a crust for this luscious, creamy white chocolate cheesecake with a bright, sweet raspberry sauce swirled throughout. It went on to become one of the bakery's top sellers, and it's as beautiful as it is delicious.

. . . .

FOR THE CRUST

Nonstick cooking spray, for greasing the pan

1¾ cups crumbs from chocolate wafer cookies

6 tablespoons unsalted butter, melted

2 tablespoons granulated sugar

FOR THE FILLING

8 ounces white chocolate, chopped

¾ cup fresh raspberries

3 tablespoons granulated sugar, plus 1½ cups

3 (8-ounce) packages cream cheese, at room temperature

1 cup sour cream, at room temperature

3 large eggs, at room temperature

2 large egg yolks, at room temperature

1½ teaspoons vanilla extract

¼ cup freshly squeezed lemon juice

. . . .

1. Preheat the oven to 325°F. Wrap the outside of a 9-inch springform pan tightly in 2 or 3 layers of heavy-duty aluminum foil. Coat the inside of the pan with cooking spray.

2. **To make the crust,** combine the cookie crumbs, butter, and sugar in a bowl and stir to mix well. Press the mixture into the bottom and a little bit up the sides of the prepared pan.

3. **To make the filling,** put the white chocolate in a microwave-safe bowl and heat in 30-second intervals, stirring in between, until completely melted and smooth.

4. In a blender or food processor, process the raspberries until they are completely pureed. Press the pureed berries through a fine-meshed sieve to remove the seeds. Stir 3 tablespoons of sugar into the raspberry juice.

5. In a large bowl, beat together the cream cheese and sour cream until well combined and smooth. Add the eggs, egg yolks, remaining 1½ cups sugar, vanilla, and lemon juice and beat to combine.

6. Using a rubber spatula, gently fold in the melted white chocolate.

7. Transfer the filling to the prepared crust. Spoon the raspberry puree on top of the cheesecake batter, dolloping it around the cake. Use a knife or a skewer to swirl the puree into the cake batter, making a pretty pattern.

8. Place the filled springform pan in a baking dish. Fill the baking dish with hot water so that the water comes about halfway up the sides of the springform pan.

9. Bake the cheesecake for 90 minutes, then turn off the oven but leave the cheesecake inside with the door closed for 45 minutes.

10. Remove the cheesecake from the oven and run a knife around the outside edge to loosen it. Let the cheesecake cool to room temperature (about 30 minutes), then cover with plastic wrap and refrigerate for at least 4 hours, until the cheesecake is completely set.

11. To serve, remove the sides of the springform pan and slice the cheesecake into wedges. Serve chilled.

TROUBLESHOOTING TIP: Every cheesecake baker wants to know one thing: how to avoid the dreaded cracks in the beautiful smooth top of your finished cake. Overbeating your batter can incorporate too much air into the mix, which may cause the cake to rise too fast while cooking and then fall, cracking the top. To avoid this, thoroughly beat together the cream cheese and sour cream, but once you've added the eggs and egg yolks, blend gently just to combine. If you end up with cracks, don't fret! Once the cake is completely chilled, heat up a knife by running it under very hot water, then dry the knife and run it gently over the crack to seal it up.

Quiche Three Ways

⇥ EACH QUICHE SERVES 6 ⇤
PREP TIME: 20 MINUTES • COOK TIME: 45 MINUTES

I made quiche every single morning in my college bakery days. Quiche Lorraine and Spinach and Mushroom Quiche were best sellers during the lunch rush. As for the Shrimp and Asparagus Quiche, I discovered this combo in Hawaii, and it has become my all-time favorite. I'll admit that I might never have thought to put these ingredients into a quiche on my own, but the result is heavenly.

PASTRY CRUST
(1 [9-INCH] PIECRUST)

1¼ cups all-purpose flour, plus additional for rolling

½ teaspoon sugar

½ teaspoon kosher salt

½ cup (1 stick) unsalted butter, very cold, cut into small cubes

3 to 4 tablespoons ice water

1. In a large bowl or a food processor, mix together the flour, sugar, and salt.
2. Cut the butter into the flour mixture either by pulsing the food processor or by hand using a pastry cutter (or two knives) until the mixture resembles a coarse meal with pea-size lumps of butter.
3. Add 2 tablespoons of ice water and stir or pulse. Add the remaining ice water a little at a time, pulsing or mixing in between, just until the mixture begins to come together. The mixture should hold together when you press it with your fingers.
4. Wrap the mixture in plastic wrap and press it into a flat disk. Refrigerate for at least 1 hour.
5. Preheat the oven to 350°F.
6. Remove the dough from the refrigerator, let it sit at room temperature for about 10 minutes, then place it on a lightly floured work surface. Using a lightly floured rolling pin, roll out the dough into a round approximately 12 inches across and ⅛ inch thick.
7. Press the pastry crust into a 9-inch pie dish. Use your fingers to pull off the excess of the pastry around the top of the pie dish.

8. Place a round of parchment paper over the bottom of the crust and add pie weights or dried beans to partially fill the shell. Parbake for 10 minutes.

9. Remove the crust from the oven and remove the pie weights and parchment paper from the pie shell.

TROUBLESHOOTING TIP: To prevent the crust from getting soggy, after parbaking the crust with the pie weights and removing the weights and parchment paper, brush the crust with a beaten egg white and then pop it back in the oven for about 5 minutes more.

QUICHE LORRAINE

4 strips bacon

1 tablespoon olive oil (or 1 tablespoon rendered bacon fat)

1 onion, thinly sliced

1 (9-inch) parbaked pastry crust

1 cup cubed Gruyère cheese

¼ cup grated Parmesan cheese

4 large eggs

2 cups heavy (whipping) cream

¼ teaspoon ground nutmeg

½ teaspoon kosher salt

¼ teaspoon freshly ground black pepper

1. Preheat the oven to 400°F.
2. In a large skillet over medium-high heat, cook the bacon until crisp. Let cool, crumble, and set aside.
3. In the same skillet, heat the oil over medium-high heat. Add the onion and cook, stirring occasionally, until softened, about 5 minutes.
4. Transfer the onions to the piecrust, spreading them in an even layer. Sprinkle the bacon and both cheeses over the crust.

5. In a medium bowl, whisk together the eggs, cream, nutmeg, salt, and pepper, then pour the mixture into the crust. Bake for about 35 minutes, until a knife inserted into the custard comes out clean.
6. Remove from the oven and set on a wire rack to cool for about 10 minutes before serving. Serve warm or at room temperature.

CONTINUED >>

SPINACH AND MUSHROOM QUICHE

4 large eggs

1½ cups heavy (whipping) cream

½ teaspoon kosher salt

¼ teaspoon freshly ground black pepper

2 cups shredded sharp white cheddar cheese

2 tablespoons olive oil

8 ounces button or cremini mushrooms, sliced

2 garlic cloves, minced

6 ounces baby spinach leaves

1 (9-inch) parbaked pastry crust

1. Preheat the oven to 400°F.
2. In a medium bowl, whisk together the eggs, cream, salt, and pepper. Stir in the cheese. Set aside.
3. Heat the oil in a skillet over medium-high heat. Add the mushrooms and cook, stirring occasionally, until softened and lightly browned, about 10 minutes.
4. Stir in the garlic, then add the spinach. Cook, stirring, just until the spinach wilts, about 2 minutes. Remove the skillet from the heat and let cool for about 10 minutes.
5. Transfer the mushroom and spinach mixture to the pastry crust and spread it evenly across the bottom. Pour the egg mixture over the top. Bake for about 35 minutes, until a knife inserted into the custard comes out clean.
6. Remove from the oven and set on a wire rack to cool for about 10 minutes before serving. Serve warm or at room temperature.

ASPARAGUS AND SHRIMP QUICHE

2 tablespoons
unsalted butter

2 small shallots, chopped

1½ cups small shrimp,
peeled and deveined

½ teaspoon kosher salt,
plus additional for seasoning the shrimp

½ teaspoon freshly ground
black pepper, plus addi-
tional for seasoning
the shrimp

4 large eggs

1½ cups heavy
(whipping) cream

½ teaspoon ground nutmeg

2 cups shredded Gruyère
cheese, divided

1 (9-inch) parbaked
pastry crust

12 asparagus tips, about
4 inches long

1. Preheat the oven to 400°F.
2. In a large skillet over medium-high heat, melt the butter. Add the shallots and cook, stirring occasionally, for about 3 minutes, until soft.
3. Add the shrimp and season with a pinch each of salt and pepper. Cook, stirring occasionally, just until the shrimp is pink and opaque, about 5 minutes. Transfer the shrimp to a plate and let cool slightly.
4. In a medium bowl, whisk together the eggs, the cream, ½ teaspoon salt, ½ teaspoon pepper, and the nutmeg. Stir in 1½ cups of the cheese and the cooked shrimp mixture.
5. Transfer the filling mixture to the crust. Sprinkle the remaining ½ cup of cheese over the top. Arrange the asparagus tips on top with the cut ends at the center and the tips pointing out like the spokes of a wheel.
6. Bake for about 35 minutes, until a knife inserted into the custard comes out clean.
7. Remove from the oven and set on a wire rack to cool for about 10 minutes before serving. Serve warm or at room temperature.

Chapter 3
SUMMER RECIPES

Red, White, and Blue Layer Cake

✷ SERVES 10 ✷

PREP TIME: 40 MINUTES, PLUS 30 MINUTES TO CHILL • COOK TIME: 25 MINUTES

*f*un fact: Summer is my favorite time for holidays! With its red, white, and blue layers and coordinating berries and sprinkles, this is the most wonderful Memorial Day or Fourth of July dessert to take to your next barbecue.

FOR THE CAKE LAYERS

Nonstick cooking spray, for greasing the pans

1½ cups (3 sticks) unsalted butter, at room temperature

3 cups granulated sugar

3 large eggs

3 large egg whites

2 teaspoons vanilla extract

3 cups all-purpose flour

2 teaspoons baking powder

¼ teaspoon kosher salt

1 cup buttermilk

Red gel food coloring

Blue gel food coloring

3 tablespoons red, white, and blue sprinkles

FOR THE FROSTING

1 cup (2 sticks) unsalted butter, at room temperature

4 to 5 cups confectioners' sugar

¼ teaspoon kosher salt

¼ cup milk

2 teaspoons vanilla extract

FOR ASSEMBLING AND DECORATING

1 cup blueberries

1 cup sliced strawberries

1¼ cups red, white, and blue sprinkles

1. **To make the cake layers,** preheat the oven to 350°F. Lightly spray three (8-inch) round cake pans with cooking spray, and line the pans with parchment paper.

2. In a large bowl using an electric mixer or in the bowl of a stand mixer, cream together the butter and sugar on medium-high speed until pale yellow and fluffy. Add the eggs, egg whites, and vanilla and beat to mix well.

3. In a medium bowl, whisk together the flour, baking powder, and salt. Add half the dry ingredients to the wet ingredients and beat to incorporate. Add the buttermilk and beat to incorporate. Add the remaining dry ingredients and beat to combine well.

4. Transfer one-third of the batter to each of two separate bowls (so that you have three bowls with equal volumes of batter). Add a few drops of red food coloring to one bowl of batter and stir to mix well. Add a few drops of blue food coloring to another bowl and mix well. Add the sprinkles to the remaining bowl of batter and stir to mix.

5. Transfer the batter to the three prepared cake pans so that you have one blue cake, one red cake, and one white cake with sprinkles. Bake for 20 to 25 minutes, until a toothpick inserted in the center comes out clean.

6. Remove the pans from the oven and set them on a wire rack to cool for a few minutes before inverting the cakes onto the wire rack to cool completely.

7. **To make the frosting,** in a medium bowl using an electric mixer or in the bowl of a stand mixer, beat the butter until creamy. Add 4 cups of confectioners' sugar gradually along with the salt, milk and vanilla and beat together until well combined. Add additional confectioners' sugar as needed to achieve the desired consistency.

8. **To assemble and decorate the cake,** use a serrated knife to level the tops of the cake layers.

9. Place the blue layer, cut-side down, on your cake plate and top it with a layer of frosting. Top the frosting with the blueberries, arranging them in a single layer.

10. Add the white layer, cut-side down, on top of the blueberries and top with a layer of frosting. Arrange the sliced strawberries in a single layer on top of the frosting.

11. Add the red layer, cut-side down, on top of the strawberries and top it with a layer of frosting.

12. Chill the cake in the refrigerator or freezer for about 30 minutes. Finish the cake by scattering the sprinkles all over the top.

13. If made ahead of time, refrigerate the cake until about 2 hours before serving and bring to room temperature to serve.

TECHNIQUE TIP: If you want to make sure that your layers are the same size, use a kitchen scale to portion the batter among the three bowls.

Mudslide Ice Cream Pie

✦ SERVES 10 ✦

PREP TIME: 30 MINUTES, PLUS 6 HOURS TO CHILL • COOK TIME: 8 MINUTES

*C*ool off this summer with this refreshing dessert that has an ice cream base in a cookie crumb crust and is topped with pecans, fudge, and whipped cream. I use coffee ice cream because I love it, but you can use any ice cream flavor you choose.

FOR THE COOKIE CRUMB CRUST

Nonstick cooking spray, for greasing the pan

20 chocolate wafer cookies

2 tablespoons granulated sugar

4 tablespoons unsalted butter, melted

FOR THE FUDGE SAUCE

4 ounces unsweetened chocolate, chopped

½ cup brown sugar

¼ cup granulated sugar

¾ cup plus 1 tablespoon heavy (whipping) cream

¼ cup light corn syrup

2 tablespoons unsalted butter

2 teaspoons vanilla extract

FOR THE FILLING

2 pints coffee ice cream

½ cup chopped pecans

FOR THE WHIPPED CREAM

1½ cups heavy (whipping) cream

¼ cup confectioners' sugar

1 teaspoon vanilla extract

½ cup chocolate syrup

1. Preheat the oven to 350°F. Coat a 9-inch pie dish with cooking spray.

2. **To make the crust,** pulse the cookies and sugar in a food processor to create fine crumbs. Add the butter and pulse just until the crumbs are thoroughly moistened.

3. Using your hands, press the crumb mixture into the bottom and up the sides of the baking dish.

4. Bake for 8 minutes, then remove from the oven and set the pan on a wire rack to cool completely.

5. **Meanwhile, make the fudge sauce.** In a microwave-safe bowl, combine the chocolate, brown sugar, granulated sugar, cream, and corn syrup. Heat in the microwave in 30- to 60-second intervals, stirring in between, until the mixture is smooth, well combined, and thick. Then whisk in the butter and vanilla.

6. Spoon half of the fudge sauce into the cookie crumb crust and spread it out in an even layer. Place the crust in the freezer for 15 minutes.

7. Let the ice cream sit on the counter for about 10 minutes to soften. Spoon the softened ice cream into the crust and use a rubber spatula to smooth it into an even layer. Place it in the freezer for 30 minutes.

8. Remove the pie from the freezer and spoon the remaining fudge sauce over the top. Sprinkle the nuts on top and put the pie back in the freezer for 1 hour.

9. **To make the whipped cream,** in a large bowl, combine the cream, confectioners' sugar, and vanilla and beat with an electric mixer until it holds stiff peaks.

10. Top the pie with the whipped cream and return it to the freezer. Freeze for at least 4 hours.

11. Serve the pie chilled, drizzled with the chocolate syrup.

SUBSTITUTION TIP: Try mint chip ice cream for more of a grasshopper pie.

Peach Upside-Down Cupcakes

*T*hese fruit-filled cupcakes are like peach cobbler taken to a whole new level. Moist, decadent, and topped with fresh peaches, they taste like little cakes made of sunshine. You can substitute just about any other fruit for the peaches—plums, nectarines, pineapple, mango, blueberries, you name it. By the way, you will never regret serving these cupcakes warm with a scoop of ice cream. I'm just saying!

Nonstick cooking spray, for greasing the pan

FOR THE PEACH TOPPING

3 tablespoons unsalted butter, melted

⅓ cup brown sugar

3 peaches, peeled, pitted, and chopped

FOR THE CUPCAKES

1½ cups all-purpose flour

1½ teaspoons baking powder

¼ teaspoon kosher salt

½ cup (1 stick) unsalted butter, at room temperature

1 cup granulated sugar

2 large eggs

2 teaspoons vanilla extract

1 peach, peeled, pitted, and finely diced

½ cup milk

1. Preheat the oven to 350°F and coat a 12-cup muffin tin with cooking spray.

2. **To make the topping,** in a small bowl, stir together the butter and brown sugar. Spoon 1½ teaspoons of the butter mixture into each muffin cup. Add the chopped peaches to the cups, dividing equally.

3. **To make the cupcakes,** in a medium bowl, combine the flour, baking powder, and salt.

4. In a large bowl using an electric mixer or in the bowl of a stand mixer, cream together the butter and sugar on high speed until pale yellow and fluffy. Add the eggs one at a time, beating until incorporated. Add the vanilla and beat until incorporated. Add half of the dry ingredients and beat on medium speed until incorporated. Scrape down the sides of the bowl, add the peaches and milk, and beat until incorporated.

Scrape down the bowl again and add the remaining dry ingredients. Beat just until incorporated.

5. Transfer the batter to the prepared muffin tin, filling each cup about two-thirds full. Bake for 18 to 20 minutes, until a toothpick inserted in the center comes out clean. Let cool in the pan for a minute or two, then transfer to a wire rack to cool completely.

6. Invert the pan onto a cutting board. Serve the cupcakes at room temperature.

TECHNIQUE TIP: I like to use a standard ice cream scoop with a sliding release to portion out cupcake batter. A standard-size scoop holds just the right amount for filling a standard muffin tin.

Fire Up the Grill Cookies

‹ MAKES 36 COOKIES ›

PREP TIME: 3 HOURS, PLUS OVERNIGHT TO SET • COOK TIME: 12 MINUTES

. . . .

These iced sugar cookies are just adorbs, and they're super fun to make, too! They look like little barbecue grills with burgers and kebabs cooking on top. What's not to love?

. . . .

FOR THE COOKIES

3 cups all-purpose flour

¾ teaspoon baking powder

¼ teaspoon kosher salt

1 cup unsalted butter, at room temperature

1 cup granulated sugar

1 large egg

1 tablespoon milk

1 teaspoon vanilla extract

FOR THE ICING

3 cups confectioners' sugar

1½ tablespoons meringue powder

4 to 6 tablespoons water

½ teaspoon vanilla extract

Black gel food coloring

Silver gel food coloring

Brown gel food coloring

Red gel food coloring

Green gel food coloring

. . . .

1. **To make the cookies,** in a medium bowl, whisk together the flour, baking powder, and salt.

2. In a large bowl using an electric mixer or in the bowl of a stand mixer, cream together the butter and sugar on medium-high speed until pale yellow and fluffy. Add the egg, milk, and vanilla and beat to combine.

3. With the mixer running on low speed, gradually add the dry ingredients, beating until the mixture is well combined and begins to pull away from the sides of the bowl. Divide the dough into two equal portions.

4. Roll out one of the dough portions between two pieces of parchment paper to ¼-inch thickness. Remove the top piece of parchment and slide the remaining piece of parchment onto a baking sheet.

5. Using a 2½-inch round cutter, cut out cookies.

6. Carefully remove the excess cookie dough from around the cutouts. (You can reroll this and use it to make more cookies.) Cover the pan with plastic wrap and chill for 1 hour. Repeat with the second portion of dough.

7. Preheat the oven to 350°F.

8. Bake the cookies for 10 to 12 minutes, until the edges are just starting to brown a bit. Transfer to a wire rack to cool completely.

9. **To make the icing,** in a large bowl using an electric mixer or in the bowl of a stand mixer, combine the confectioners' sugar and meringue powder. Add 4 tablespoons of water and the vanilla and, with the mixer set on low speed, beat to combine. Add additional water as needed to achieve the right consistency. The icing should be fairly thick and very smooth. Raise the speed of the mixer gradually and beat until the icing is thick and glossy.

10. Put half of the icing in one bowl and add several drops of black food coloring. Divide the remaining icing among four bowls for the other colors. Mix in a few drops of each food coloring to a separate bowl to achieve your desired shade, keeping in mind that the color will darken a bit as the icing dries. Cover the silver, brown, red, and green icings with plastic wrap and refrigerate.

11. Put the black icing in a piping bag fitted with a small round tip and pipe a thin outline of icing around the outside edge of each cookie.

12. Return the black icing to the bowl, add about ½ to 1 teaspoon of water and stir to mix, thinning out the icing a bit. Transfer the frosting back to the same piping bag.

13. Use the thinned out black icing to "flood" the top of the cookie inside the icing outline. You can use a toothpick to spread the icing into any missed spots. Let dry for 1 hour.

14. Put the silver icing in a piping bag fitted with a small round tip and pipe a circle on top of the black icing to make the outside ring of a grill. Next, pipe lines across the circle to make the grill bars. Let the cookies stand, uncovered, overnight to dry and set.

15. Put the other icing colors in piping bags fitted with small round tips. Use the brown icing to pipe a few burger shapes on top of each cookie. You can also use the brown icing to pipe a few skewers on the grill. Then use the red and green icing to pipe vegetables on the skewers (or you can just pipe some vegetables on the grill without the skewers).

16. Let the cookies stand, uncovered, for 1 hour to dry.

Giant Chocolate Chip Cookie Ice Cream Sandwich

⤳ SERVES 10 ⤶

PREP TIME: 45 MINUTES, PLUS OVERNIGHT TO CHILL • COOK TIME: 15 MINUTES

* * * * * * * * * * * * * * * * * * * *

*T*his ginormous, amazing, showstopping dessert is ideal for birthdays or any summer celebration. You're going to want to eat it all by yourself, but don't. Or, on second thought, I dare you to!

* * * * * * * * * * * * * * * * * * * *

Nonstick cooking spray, for greasing the pans

¾ cup (1½ sticks) unsalted butter, at room temperature

¾ cup brown sugar

¾ cup granulated sugar

2 large eggs

2 teaspoons vanilla extract

2¼ cups all-purpose flour

1 teaspoon baking soda

½ teaspoon kosher salt

1 (12-ounce) package semi-sweet chocolate chips

1½ quarts vanilla bean ice cream

1 cup mini chocolate chips or chopped nuts for decorating

* * * * * * * * * * * * * * * * * * * *

1. Preheat the oven to 350°F. Coat two (9-inch) springform pans with cooking spray and line them with parchment paper.

2. In a large bowl using an electric mixer or in the bowl of a stand mixer, cream together the butter and sugars on medium speed until pale yellow and fluffy. Add the eggs and vanilla and beat to combine. Add the flour, baking soda, and salt and beat to fully incorporate. Stir in the chocolate chips.

3. Divide the dough into two equal portions and press one portion into each

of the prepared pans in an even layer. Bake for about 15 minutes, until the edges are golden brown.

4. Remove the pans from the oven and set them on a wire rack to cool.

5. Remove the ice cream from the freezer and let it stand on the countertop to soften for about 15 minutes.

6. When the cookies are completely cooled, carefully detach the sides of the pans and remove the cookies.

7. Reattach the sides of one of the pans and place one cookie in it, top-side down.

8. Add the softened ice cream on top of the cookie in the pan and use a rubber spatula to smooth it into an even layer. Place the other cookie on top, top-side up, and press down so that it is flat. Cover with plastic wrap and freeze overnight.

9. To serve, remove the springform pan and press the mini chocolate chips or nuts into the ice cream all the way around the sides. Cut the ice cream sandwich into wedges and serve.

SUBSTITUTION TIP: Vanilla ice cream is a classic ice cream sandwich filler, but you can use any type you like. Try chocolate, coffee, or butter brickle for variation.

Pink Lemonade Bars

PREP TIME: 30 MINUTES, PLUS 30 MINUTES TO CHILL • COOK TIME: 40 MINUTES

How do you make lemon bars even better? Turn them pink, obviously! These bars—inspired by one of my favorite drinks—have a buttery base layered with a delicate raspberry-lemon filling and are dusted with confectioners' sugar. Make these bad boys and enjoy a refreshing summertime treat.

FOR THE CRUST

Nonstick cooking spray, for greasing the pan

¾ cup plus 2 tablespoons all-purpose flour

½ cup confectioners' sugar

½ teaspoon kosher salt

½ teaspoon lemon zest

6 tablespoons unsalted butter, at room temperature, cut into pieces

FOR THE FILLING

1 cup fresh raspberries

2 large eggs

¾ cup granulated sugar

¼ cup plus 1 tablespoon freshly squeezed lemon juice

⅛ teaspoon kosher salt

2 tablespoons all-purpose flour

Confectioners' sugar, for sprinkling

1. **To make the crust,** coat an 8-inch square baking pan with cooking spray. Line the pan with a parchment paper sling and coat the parchment with cooking spray.

2. In a food processor, pulse together the flour, confectioners' sugar, salt, and lemon zest. Add the butter and pulse until the mixture comes together into a dough.

3. Press the dough into the bottom and about ½ inch up the sides of the prepared pan. Refrigerate for 30 minutes.

4. Preheat the oven to 350°F.

5. Prick the dough in several places with a fork. Bake for about 20 minutes, until the crust is golden brown, then remove from the oven, leaving the oven on.

6. **While the crust is baking, make the filling.** Put the raspberries in a food processor or blender and process to a smooth puree. Press the puree through a fine-mesh sieve to remove the seeds.

7. In a medium bowl, whisk together the eggs, granulated sugar, and lemon juice. Whisk in the raspberry puree and salt. Add the flour and whisk to combine.

8. Pour the filling mixture on top of the crust. Bake for about 20 minutes more, until the filling is set and beginning to brown around the edges.

9. Remove the pan from the oven and set it on a wire rack. Let cool completely in the pan.

10. Run a knife around the edge to loosen, then use the parchment paper sling to lift the bars out of the pan. Cut into 16 squares. Sprinkle confectioners' sugar over the top and serve.

SUBSTITUTION TIP: If you don't have fresh raspberries, you can substitute strawberries or other fresh or frozen berries.

S'mores Sandwich Cookies

✦ MAKES 8 SANDWICH COOKIES ✦

PREP TIME: 40 MINUTES, PLUS 15 MINUTES TO CHILL • COOK TIME: 10 MINUTES

I've got great memories of making s'mores by a campfire on a hot summer night, but I'm telling you, these are even better. They involve toasted marshmallows sandwiched between chocolate-coated, graham cracker–flavored cookies—all the flavors you love from the original, but you don't have to fight mosquitoes or sleep on the ground to enjoy them!

2 cups graham cracker crumbs (from about 15 whole graham cracker sheets)

¼ cup granulated sugar

2 tablespoons packed dark brown sugar

½ teaspoon baking soda

¼ teaspoon kosher salt

6 tablespoons unsalted butter, melted and cooled

1 large egg, lightly beaten

½ teaspoon vanilla extract

8 ounces semisweet chocolate, chopped

8 jumbo marshmallows

1. Preheat the oven to 350°F and line a baking sheet with parchment paper.

2. In a large bowl, whisk together the graham cracker crumbs, granulated sugar, brown sugar, baking soda, and salt. Add the butter, egg, and vanilla and mix until well combined.

3. Form the dough into 1½-inch balls and place them on the prepared baking sheet, about 2 inches apart.

4. Bake for 8 to 10 minutes, until lightly browned. Remove the baking sheet from the oven and let the cookies cool for about 5 minutes before transferring them to a wire rack to cool completely.

5. Put the chocolate in a microwave-safe bowl and heat in 30-second intervals, stirring in between, until melted and smooth.

CONTINUED >>

6. Place the cookies on a baking sheet upside down (so that the flat side of each cookie is facing up). Use a pastry brush to brush a layer of melted chocolate over each cookie. Refrigerate for 15 minutes to allow the chocolate to set.

7. Put the marshmallows on skewers and toast them lightly over a flame.

8. Put 1 marshmallow on the chocolate side of each of 8 cookies and then top each with one of the remaining cookies, chocolate-side down.

9. Serve immediately.

TECHNIQUE TIP: You can toast the marshmallows directly over the flame of a gas stovetop burner or use a culinary torch. Alternatively, arrange the marshmallows on squares of parchment paper on a baking sheet and toast under the broiler for about 2 minutes, being sure to watch them carefully so that they don't burn.

Plum and Almond Tart

SERVES 8

PREP TIME: 30 MINUTES, PLUS 1 HOUR TO CHILL • COOK TIME: 50 MINUTES

*N*ow, I know what you're thinking: What the heck is this recipe about? The answer is frangipane, a lovely French almond pastry cream, layered on a buttery-crisp crust and topped with juicy sliced plums.

FOR THE CRUST

1¼ cups all-purpose flour, plus additional for rolling

2 teaspoons granulated sugar

½ teaspoon kosher salt

½ cup (1 stick) unsalted butter, very cold, cut into small cubes

3 to 4 tablespoons ice water

Nonstick cooking spray, for greasing the pan

FOR THE FILLING

½ cup (1 stick) unsalted butter, at room temperature

½ cup superfine sugar

2 large eggs, lightly beaten

2 teaspoons vanilla extract

½ cup all-purpose flour

1¼ cups coarsely ground almond meal

10 plums, pitted and sliced into thin wedges

1. **To make the crust,** in a medium bowl or food processor, mix together the flour, sugar, and salt.
2. Cut the butter into the flour mixture either by pulsing the food processor or by hand using a pastry cutter (or two knives) until the mixture resembles a coarse meal with pea-size lumps of butter.
3. Add 2 tablespoons of ice water and stir or pulse. Add the remaining ice water a little at a time, pulsing or mixing in between, just until the mixture begins to come together. The mixture should hold together when you press it with your fingers.
4. Wrap the mixture in plastic wrap and press it into a disk. Refrigerate for at least 1 hour.
5. Preheat the oven to 350°F. Lightly coat a 9-inch removable-bottom tart pan with cooking spray.
6. Remove the dough from the refrigerator, let it sit at room temperature for about 10 minutes, then place it on a lightly floured work surface. Using a lightly floured rolling pin, roll out the dough into a round approximately 12 inches across and ⅛ inch thick.

CONTINUED >>

7. Press the pastry dough into the prepared tart pan. Trim off the excess dough around the edges and save it for decoration or discard. Use your fingers to flute the rim of the pastry around the top of the pan. Put the crust in the refrigerator while you make the filling.

8. **To make the filling,** in a large bowl using an electric mixer or in the bowl of a stand mixer, cream together the butter and sugar on medium-high speed until pale yellow and fluffy. Add the eggs and vanilla and beat to incorporate.

9. Stir together the flour and almond meal and gently fold into the butter mixture until well combined.

10. Remove the tart shell from the refrigerator and spoon the filling into it, spreading it into an even layer.

11. Arrange the plum slices in concentric circles on top of the filling, pressing down slightly to nestle them into the filling.

12. Bake the tart for 45 to 50 minutes, until the pastry is golden and crisp and the filling is set.

13. Remove the pan from the oven and set it on a wire rack to cool for 15 minutes before removing the tart from the tin. Serve at room temperature.

MAKE AHEAD TIP: Pastry dough keeps really well in the freezer. You can wrap it tightly in step 4 with a double layer of plastic wrap and place it in a freezer-safe resealable plastic bag. To cook it, let it come to room temperature by letting it sit out on the countertop for about 30 minutes, then proceed with the recipe starting with step 5.

Strawberry Shortcake Parfaits

✦ MAKES 12 ✦

PREP TIME: **30 MINUTES** • COOK TIME: **24 MINUTES**

*T*hese parfaits are portable, cute, and great for summer. Sweet strawberries and fluffy whipped cream are layered with tender shortcake in mason jars for a tasty take-along treat.

FOR THE SHORTCAKES

Nonstick cooking spray, for greasing the pan

2 cups all-purpose flour, plus additional for dusting the pan

3 tablespoons cornstarch

½ teaspoon kosher salt

½ teaspoon baking powder

½ teaspoon baking soda

¾ cup (1½ sticks) unsalted butter, at room temperature

1½ cups granulated sugar

½ teaspoon lemon zest

4 large eggs

1½ teaspoons vanilla extract

1 cup sour cream

FOR THE FILLING LAYERS

2 pounds fresh strawberries, diced, plus 12 more small whole strawberries for garnish

¼ cup granulated sugar

2 cups heavy (whipping) cream

½ cup confectioners' sugar

1. **To make the shortcakes,** preheat the oven to 350°F. Coat a rimmed half baking sheet (18 by 13 inches) with cooking spray and dust it with flour.

2. In a medium bowl, whisk together the flour, cornstarch, salt, baking powder, and baking soda.

3. In a large bowl using an electric mixer or in the bowl of a stand mixer, cream together the butter, sugar, and lemon zest on medium-high speed until pale yellow and fluffy. Add the eggs one at a time, beating after each addition to incorporate. Add the vanilla and beat to incorporate.

4. Add half of the dry ingredients and beat just until incorporated. Add the sour cream and mix until combined. Add the remaining dry ingredients and beat again just until incorporated.

5. Transfer the batter to the prepared baking sheet. Bake for 20 to 24 minutes, until a toothpick inserted in the center comes out clean.

6. Remove the pan from the oven and set it on a wire rack to cool completely.

7. Use a 2-inch round biscuit cutter to cut out 24 rounds of shortcake.

8. **To make the filling layers,** place the diced strawberries in a medium bowl and sprinkle the sugar over the top. Toss to mix and let stand for 10 minutes.

9. In a large bowl, combine the cream and confectioners' sugar and beat with an electric mixer on medium-high speed until the mixture holds stiff peaks.

10. **To assemble the parfaits,** put one cake round on the bottom of each of 12 half-pint mason jars or dessert glasses. Spoon some strawberries over each and then dollop whipped cream on top. Repeat with the remaining cake rounds, strawberries, and whipped cream. Top each parfait with 1 whole strawberry and serve immediately or refrigerate until ready to serve.

Jalapeño-Cheese Corn Muffins

☙ MAKES 12 MUFFINS ❧
PREP TIME: **20 MINUTES** • COOK TIME: **18 MINUTES**

*A*s a Texan, I have to rep this recipe. Our official state pepper—yes, we have one—is the jalapeño. I love this recipe because it is easy to make in a single bowl, it goes with just about everything, and, oh yes, it's loaded with delicious cheese and spicy jalapeños. Ooo-wee!

Nonstick cooking spray, for greasing the pan

1 cup cornmeal

1 cup all-purpose flour

1 teaspoon baking powder

½ teaspoon baking soda

½ teaspoon kosher salt

1 cup buttermilk

½ cup (1 stick) unsalted butter, melted

½ cup granulated sugar

2 large eggs

2 tablespoons honey

¼ cup shredded cheddar cheese

2 jalapeño peppers, seeded and diced

1. Preheat the oven to 375°F and coat a 12-cup muffin tin with cooking spray.
2. In a large bowl, whisk together the cornmeal, flour, baking powder, baking soda, and salt.
3. In a medium bowl, stir together the buttermilk, butter, sugar, eggs, and honey. Add the wet ingredients to the dry ingredients and stir until thoroughly moistened. Stir in the cheese and jalapeños.
4. Scoop the batter into the prepared muffin tin, filling each about three-fourths full. Bake for 16 to 18 minutes, until a toothpick inserted in the center comes out clean.
5. Remove the pan from the oven and let the muffins cool for a couple of minutes in the pan before transferring them to a wire rack to cool completely.
6. Serve warm or at room temperature.

Focaccia with Cherry Tomatoes and Basil

❖ SERVES 8 ❖

PREP TIME: 30 MINUTES, PLUS 1 HOUR 30 MINUTES TO PROOF AND RISE
COOK TIME: 20 MINUTES

This Italian olive oil bread is similar to pizza crust and can be used to make sandwiches or eaten on its own. I first made this recipe when I was in culinary school, topping the flavorful bread with bright cherry tomatoes and fresh basil. It has since become my favorite summer snack or appetizer.

1 cup warm water

1 envelope (2¼ teaspoons) active dry yeast

¼ teaspoon sugar

2½ cups all-purpose flour, divided, plus more for rolling

½ cup extra-virgin olive oil, divided, plus additional for greasing

½ teaspoon kosher salt

1 pint cherry tomatoes, halved

¼ cup chopped fresh basil

1. In a large bowl, stir together the water, yeast, and sugar. Let the mixture stand for 10 minutes, until frothy.

2. Stir 1 cup of flour and ¼ cup of oil into the yeast mixture. Let stand for 5 minutes more.

3. Add the remaining 1½ cups of flour and the salt and stir until the mixture comes together into a shaggy dough. Turn out the dough onto a lightly floured work surface and knead until smooth, about 12 to 15 times.

4. Lightly oil a large bowl and place the dough in it, turning it to coat with the oil. Cover with a clean dish towel and set in a warm spot on your countertop (or in your oven with the light on) and let rise until doubled in size, about 1 hour.

5. Preheat the oven to 450°F.

6. Oil a rimmed quarter baking sheet (9 by 13 inches) with 2 tablespoons of the remaining olive oil. Place the dough on the oiled baking sheet and

push it into a flat layer, pressing it into the corners.

7. Add the tomatoes, arranging them cut-side up on top of the dough and pressing them in slightly. Drizzle the remaining 2 tablespoons of olive oil over the top. Let the dough rise again until it puffs up a bit, about 20 minutes, then bake for 15 to 20 minutes, until golden brown.

8. Remove from the oven and immediately scatter the basil over the top. Let cool for at least 15 minutes before slicing.

ADVANCED TIP: Scatter chopped fresh herbs—such as basil, oregano, or rosemary—on top of the dough, pressing them down slightly so that they stick, before baking.

Ginger Pumpkin Pie, page 89

Spooky Graveyard Cake

⚜ SERVES 12 ⚜

PREP TIME: **1 HOUR** • COOK TIME: **45 MINUTES**

*E*ven though the name says this cake is spooky, it's cute, too! It's perfect for a Halloween party, easy to make, and fun to decorate. You can add your own embellishments, like gummy worms, candy eyeballs, or crumbled chocolate cookie "dirt." Kids will enjoy helping decorate it as much as they will love eating it!

FOR THE CAKE

Butter and flour or cooking spray, for preparing the pan

2 cups all-purpose flour

2 cups granulated sugar

¾ cup unsweetened cocoa powder

2 teaspoons baking soda

1 teaspoon baking powder

1 teaspoon kosher salt

1 cup vegetable oil

1 cup hot coffee

1 cup milk

2 large eggs

1 teaspoon vanilla extract

FOR THE FROSTING

½ cup (1 stick) unsalted butter, at room temperature

2½ cups confectioners' sugar

¾ cup unsweetened cocoa powder

2 to 4 tablespoons heavy (whipping) cream

2 teaspoons vanilla extract

Pinch kosher salt

FOR DECORATING

6 ounces dark chocolate

White writing icing

8 ounces chocolate wafer cookies, crushed (about 2 cups)

1. **To make the cake,** preheat the oven to 325°F. Coat a 9-by-13-inch baking pan with butter or cooking spray and dust it with flour.

2. In a large bowl using an electric mixer or in the bowl of a stand mixer, stir together the flour, sugar, cocoa, baking soda, baking powder, and salt on low speed.

3. Add the oil, coffee, and milk and beat on medium speed for 2 minutes. Add the eggs and vanilla and beat for 2 minutes more.

4. Transfer the batter to the prepared baking pan. Bake for about 45 minutes, until a toothpick inserted in the center comes out clean.

5. **To make the frosting,** in a large bowl using an electric mixer or in the bowl of a stand mixer, beat the butter for 1 minute on medium speed until smooth.

6. Add the confectioners' sugar and cocoa and beat to combine. With the mixer on low speed, add 2 tablespoons of cream and the vanilla and salt and beat to combine.

7. Raise the mixer speed to high and continue to beat until the mixture reaches the desired consistency, 2 to 4 minutes. Add an additional 1 to 2 tablespoons of cream, as needed, to achieve the right consistency.

8. **To make the decorations,** place the chocolate in a microwave-safe bowl and heat on 50 percent power in 30-second intervals, stirring in between, until it is melted and smooth.

9. On a large piece of parchment paper, draw 12 tombstone shapes—a rectangle with a rounded top, about 2½ inches tall and 1½ inches wide. Turn the paper over so that the drawing is on the bottom (you'll be able to see the outline through the paper) and lay it flat on a baking sheet. Drop a spoonful of the melted chocolate onto one of the tombstone outlines and use the back of the spoon to spread it out to fill the outline. Repeat to fill all 12 of the tombstone outlines, then put the baking sheet in the refrigerator or freezer to chill for about 10 minutes. When the chocolate has set, use the white writing icing to write "RIP" or other "spooky" words on the tombstones. Refrigerate again to let the icing set.

10. When the cake is completely cooled, spread the frosting over the top in an even layer. Sprinkle the cookie crumbs on top in an even layer. Arrange the tombstones on the cake, sticking them into the top so that they stand up like headstones in a graveyard.

> **ADVANCED TIP:** If you're feeling creative, dress up your graveyard. Try putting melted chocolate in a piping bag and piping a tree, make fondant zombie hands sticking up out of the graves, or use a special piping tip and green frosting to make tufts of grass.

Trick-or-Treat Cookies

→ MAKES 12 COOKIES ←

PREP TIME: 30 MINUTES, PLUS 2 HOURS TO CHILL AND OVERNIGHT TO SET

COOK TIME: 12 MINUTES

Trick-or-Treat Cookies are jack-o'-lantern cookies filled with candy that capture all the fun of Halloween—one of my favorite holidays! The base of this recipe is a classic sugar cookie dough that turns out tender, holds its shape in the oven, and has just the right balance of sweet, buttery goodness.

FOR THE COOKIES

3 cups all-purpose flour

¾ teaspoon baking powder

¼ teaspoon salt

1 cup (2 sticks) unsalted butter, at room temperature

1 cup granulated sugar

1 large egg

1 tablespoon milk

1 teaspoon vanilla extract

Confectioners' sugar, for rolling out the dough

1½ cups small candies, for filling the cookies

FOR THE ICING "GLUE"

1 cup confectioners' sugar

2 to 4 tablespoons milk

FOR THE ROYAL ICING

3 cups confectioners' sugar

1½ tablespoons meringue powder

4 to 6 tablespoons water

½ teaspoon vanilla extract

Orange gel food coloring

Green gel food coloring

FOR DECORATING

Black writing icing (optional)

1. **To make the cookies,** in a medium bowl, whisk together the flour, baking powder, and salt.

2. In a large bowl using an electric mixer or in the bowl of a stand mixer, cream together the butter and sugar on medium-high speed until pale yellow and fluffy. Add the egg, milk, and vanilla and beat to combine.

3. With the mixer running on low speed, gradually add the dry ingredients, beating until the mixture is well combined and begins to pull away from the sides of the bowl. Divide the dough into three equal portions.

4. Using a rolling pin lightly dusted with confectioners' sugar, roll out two of the dough portions between two pieces of parchment paper to ¼-inch thickness to make 24 whole pumpkins. Use the remaining portion to make the middle pieces. Remove the top piece of parchment and slide the remaining piece of parchment onto a baking sheet. Use a pumpkin-shaped cookie cutter to cut out 12 cookies.

5. Carefully remove the excess dough from around the cutouts. (You can reroll this and use it to make more cookies.) Cover the pan with plastic wrap and chill for 1 hour.

6. **To make the middle piece of the cookies,** roll out the remaining portion of dough between two sheets of parchment paper to about ½-inch thickness. (The middle layer should be thicker than the top and bottom layers.)

7. Remove the top sheet of parchment and slide the remaining piece of parchment onto a baking sheet. Cut out 12 pumpkin shapes. Next, use a small round cutter to cut out the centers of the pumpkins (make two round cuts in each pumpkin if necessary), leaving the outline of a pumpkin.

8. Carefully remove the excess cookie dough from around the cutouts and from the middles of the cutouts. (You can reroll this and use it to make more cookies.) Cover the pan with plastic wrap and chill for 1 hour.

9. Preheat the oven to 375°F.

10. Bake the full pumpkin cookies for about 10 minutes, until they are crisp and just beginning to brown on the bottom. Remove from the oven and let cool on the pan for a few minutes before transferring to a rack to cool completely.

11. Bake the pumpkin outline cutouts for about 12 minutes, until they are set and just beginning to brown. Remove from the oven and let cool on the pan for a few minutes before transferring to a rack to cool completely.

12. **To make the icing "glue,"** combine the confectioners' sugar and 2 tablespoons of milk and stir until smooth, adding the remaining milk gradually until the right consistency is reached. Transfer the mixture to a piping bag fitted with a small round tip or put it into a sturdy resealable plastic bag and snip off a very small bit of the corner to make a piping bag.

13. Place half of the pumpkin cookies on a platter and then pipe a line of the icing glue all the way around the edge. Lay a pumpkin cutout (middle) cookie on top so that the icing glue adheres it to the bottom cookie. Fill the hole with candies. Pipe a line of icing glue around the cutout layer and then place another pumpkin cookie on top, sealing in the candy.

CONTINUED >>

14. **To make the royal icing,** in a large bowl using an electric mixer or in the bowl of a stand mixer, combine the confectioners' sugar and meringue powder. Add 4 tablespoons of water and the vanilla and beat on low speed to combine. Add additional water as needed, a tablespoon at a time, to achieve the right consistency. Raise the speed of the mixer gradually and beat until the icing is thick and glossy.

15. Place one-third of the mixture in a small bowl and stir in 2 drops of green gel food coloring until well combined. Add a bit of water if the mixture is too thick.

16. Add 3 to 4 drops of orange gel food coloring to the larger portion of icing and mix to combine well. Add a bit of water if the mixture is too thick.

17. Spoon the icing into piping bags fitted with small round tips or sturdy resealable plastic bags with the corners snipped off to make piping bags.

18. Pipe the orange icing onto the main part of the pumpkin cookies. Use the green icing to color the stem. Let the icing set overnight.

19. If desired, use the black writing icing to draw jack-o'-lantern faces on the pumpkins.

ADVANCED TIP: You can use multiple shapes for your cookies—coffins, ghosts, or mummies are all fun ideas. Use royal icing, candy eyeballs, and other decorations to decorate the tops appropriately.

Pumpkin Swirl Brownies

❖ MAKES 16 BROWNIES ❖

PREP TIME: **15 MINUTES** • COOK TIME: **45 MINUTES**

*W*elcome the fall season by combining two favorite ingredients—pumpkin and chocolate—into one rich, fudgy brownie. The pumpkin pie spice draws out the sweetness of the pumpkin and adds depth to the rich chocolate.

½ cup (1 stick) unsalted butter, plus additional for greasing the pan

6 ounces dark chocolate, chopped

2 cups all-purpose flour

1 teaspoon baking powder

¼ teaspoon kosher salt

1½ cups granulated sugar

4 large eggs

2 teaspoons vanilla extract

1¼ cups pumpkin puree

¼ cup vegetable oil

1½ teaspoons pumpkin pie spice

1. Preheat the oven to 350°F. Butter a 9-inch square baking pan, line the pan with a parchment paper sling, and butter the paper.
2. Place the butter and chocolate in a microwave-safe bowl and heat in 30-second intervals, stirring in between, until completely melted and smooth.
3. In a medium bowl, combine the flour, baking powder, and salt.
4. In a large bowl using an electric mixer or in the bowl of a stand mixer, combine the sugar, eggs, and vanilla and beat on medium-high speed for 3 to 5 minutes until fluffy and well combined. Add the dry ingredients to the wet ingredients and beat to combine.
5. Transfer half the batter to a separate bowl, then add the melted chocolate and stir to incorporate.
6. Add the pumpkin, oil, and pumpkin pie spice to the other bowl and stir to mix well.
7. Spoon half the chocolate batter into the prepared baking pan. Add half the pumpkin batter on top. Finish with the remaining chocolate batter and then the remaining pumpkin batter.
8. Use a butter knife or a rubber spatula to swirl together the pumpkin and chocolate batters in a marbled pattern. Bake for 40 to 45 minutes, until the brownies are set on top.
9. Remove the pan from the oven and set it on a wire rack to cool completely. Cut into squares and serve at room temperature.

Toffee Pecan Cake

SERVES 10

PREP TIME: 30 MINUTES • COOK TIME: 40 MINUTES

*T*his cake recipe is ah-mazing. It's moist, buttery, and decadent, with toasted pecans and delicious crunchy bits of toffee throughout. And that glaze? Oh. My. Goodness. This is a must-have fall cake. You just have to try it.

FOR THE CAKE

Nonstick cooking spray, for greasing the pan

2 cups all-purpose flour

2 teaspoons baking powder

¾ teaspoon kosher salt

2 cups granulated sugar

1 cup (2 sticks) unsalted butter, at room temperature

3 large eggs

1 teaspoon vanilla extract

1 cup buttermilk

1 cup finely chopped toasted pecans

½ cup toffee bits

FOR THE TOFFEE GLAZE

½ cup unsalted butter

½ cup heavy (whipping) cream

1 cup dark brown sugar

½ teaspoon vanilla extract

Pinch kosher salt

1. **To make the cake,** preheat the oven to 350°F and coat a Bundt pan with cooking spray.
2. In a medium bowl, whisk together the flour, baking powder, and salt.
3. In a large bowl using an electric mixer or in the bowl of a stand mixer, cream together the sugar and butter on medium-high speed until smooth and fluffy, about 4 minutes. Reduce the mixer speed to medium and add the eggs one at a time, beating after each addition to incorporate.
4. Add the vanilla and then add the flour mixture in three batches, alternating with the buttermilk and ending with the flour, mixing after each addition to combine. Using a rubber spatula, gently stir in the pecans and toffee.
5. Transfer the batter to the prepared cake pan. Bake for 35 to 40 minutes, until a toothpick inserted in the center comes out clean.
6. Remove the pan from the oven and let the cake cool for about 10 minutes

before inverting it onto a cake platter and letting it cool completely.

7. **While the cake is cooling, make the toffee glaze.** Melt the butter in a heavy saucepan over medium-high heat. Add the cream and brown sugar and bring the mixture to a boil. Lower the heat to medium and cook, stirring constantly, until the mixture is thickened, 6 to 8 minutes. Add the vanilla and salt and mix to incorporate.

8. Just before serving, drizzle the glaze generously over the cake.

MAKE AHEAD TIP: You can make the cake and the glaze a day ahead of time, but don't glaze the cake until just before serving. Keep the cake uncovered at room temperature and the glaze refrigerated. Warm the glaze in the microwave to bring it back to pourable consistency, and pour it over the cake right before you serve.

Baked Apple Cider Donuts

❖ MAKES 12 DONUTS ❖

PREP TIME: **15 MINUTES** • COOK TIME: **10 MINUTES**

I love the idea of a baked donut because it's a little healthier and easier to make. The apple cider gives these tons of flavor, and the buttermilk makes them delectably moist. The flavors here are everything I love about fall baking.

FOR THE DONUTS

Nonstick cooking spray, for greasing the pan

2 cups all-purpose flour

1 teaspoon baking soda

¾ teaspoon baking powder

1½ teaspoons ground cinnamon

¼ teaspoon ground nutmeg

¼ teaspoon kosher salt

½ cup apple cider

½ cup brown sugar

½ cup granulated sugar

½ cup buttermilk, at room temperature

1 large egg, at room temperature

2 tablespoons unsalted butter, melted

1 teaspoon vanilla extract

FOR THE TOPPING

1 cup granulated sugar

1 teaspoon ground cinnamon

6 tablespoons unsalted butter, melted

1. **To make the donuts,** preheat the oven to 350°F and coat two (6-cavity) donut pans with cooking spray.

2. In a large bowl, whisk together the flour, baking soda, baking powder, cinnamon, nutmeg, and salt.

3. In a medium bowl, whisk together the cider, brown sugar, granulated sugar, buttermilk, egg, butter, and vanilla.

4. Add the wet ingredients to the dry ingredients and stir to combine well.

5. Transfer the batter to a piping bag fitted with a round tip, or use a large, resealable plastic bag and snip off one corner. Pipe the batter into the prepared pan, filling each donut cavity about half full.

6. Bake until the donuts begin to brown around the edges and spring back when pressed, about 10 minutes.

7. Remove the pan from the oven and let the donuts cool in the pan for a couple

CONTINUED >>

of minutes before transferring them to a wire rack.

8. **To make the topping,** in a small bowl, stir together the sugar and cinnamon.

9. After removing the donuts from the pan, brush each with the melted butter and then dunk them in the cinnamon-sugar mixture.

TROUBLESHOOTING TIP: If you don't have a donut pan, no worries— just make 12 apple cider donut muffins instead. Grease a standard 12-cup muffin tin and fill each cup about three-fourths full. Bake for about 18 minutes.

ADVANCED TIP: For even more apple cider flavor, start with 1½ cups apple cider and simmer it in a saucepan for about 20 minutes, until it is reduced to ½ cup. Substitute this for the apple cider in the recipe.

Ginger Pumpkin Pie

❖ SERVES 10 ❖

PREP TIME: **20 MINUTES** • COOK TIME: **1 HOUR 5 MINUTES**

*Y*ou can't celebrate the fall season without having some pumpkin pie, can you? The gingersnap cookie crumb crust on this version takes it to a whole new level. You might want to go a little crazy and try swapping pureed sweet potatoes for the pumpkin. Heaven.

FOR THE CRUST

3½ cups gingersnap cookie crumbs (from about 24 cookies)

6 tablespoons unsalted butter, melted

FOR THE FILLING

2 large eggs, at room temperature

1 large egg yolk, at room temperature

1 (15-ounce) can pumpkin puree

1¼ cups heavy (whipping) cream

⅔ cup brown sugar

1½ teaspoons pumpkin pie spice

1 teaspoon minced fresh ginger

1 teaspoon molasses

1. **To make the crust,** preheat the oven to 350°F.
2. In a large bowl, combine the cookie crumbs and melted butter and toss to mix thoroughly. Transfer the mixture to a 9-inch pie dish and press it into the bottom and up the sides in an even layer.
3. Bake the crust until firm, 20 to 25 minutes. Remove from the oven and let cool while you make the filling. Raise the oven heat to 375°F.
4. **To make the filling,** in a large bowl, combine the eggs, egg yolk, pumpkin, cream, brown sugar, pumpkin pie spice, ginger, and molasses and stir with a spoon to mix well. Pour the mixture into the prepared crust.
5. Bake for 55 to 60 minutes, until the filling is set and a toothpick inserted in the center comes out clean.
6. Remove from the oven and set on a wire rack to cool. Serve at room temperature.

TECHNIQUE TIP: If you don't have a food processor to make cookie crumbs, you can put the cookies in a resealable plastic bag and smash them with a meat tenderizer or other heavy object.

Black Friday Black Forest Cake

⇥ SERVES 10 ⇤

PREP TIME: **30 MINUTES** • COOK TIME: **35 MINUTES**

I don't know about you, but I am all in for Black Friday. After I eat my delicious Thanksgiving dinner, I am at the store ready to shop! This recipe captures the decadence of a shopping spree, with a rich chocolate cake, luscious cherry filling, and luxurious whipped cream topping.

FOR THE CAKE

Nonstick cooking spray, for greasing the pans

2 cups granulated sugar

1¾ cups all-purpose flour

¾ cup unsweetened cocoa powder

1½ teaspoons baking powder

1½ teaspoons baking soda

1 teaspoon kosher salt

2 large eggs

1 cup buttermilk

½ cup vegetable oil

2 teaspoons vanilla extract

1 cup boiling water

FOR THE FILLING

¼ cup granulated sugar

2 tablespoons cornstarch

2 tablespoons cherry liqueur

1½ cups frozen pitted cherries, thawed and quartered

FOR THE WHIPPED CREAM AND TOPPING

3¾ cups heavy (whipping) cream

2 cups confectioners' sugar

1 tablespoon vanilla extract

1 (4-ounce) bar bittersweet chocolate

½ cup cherries, thawed

1. **To make the cake,** preheat the oven to 350°F. and coat two (9-inch) round cake pans with cooking spray.

2. In a large bowl using an electric mixer or the bowl of a stand mixer, combine the sugar, flour, cocoa, baking powder, baking soda, and salt and stir to mix.

3. Add the eggs, buttermilk, oil, and vanilla and beat on medium speed for 2 minutes.

4. Add the boiling water and stir to mix well. Pour the batter evenly into the prepared cake pans.

5. Bake for 30 to 35 minutes, until the cakes spring back when pressed and a toothpick inserted in the center comes out clean.

6. Remove the pans from the oven and set them on a wire rack to cool for about 15 minutes. Run a knife around the outside edge of each cake to loosen it, then invert it onto a cutting board or plate. Use a serrated knife to level the tops of the cakes.

CONTINUED >>

7. **To make the filling,** in a medium saucepan, stir together the sugar, cornstarch, and liqueur. Cook over medium heat, stirring occasionally, until the sugar dissolves.

8. Add the cherries and stir to incorporate. Continue to cook until the cherries begin to break down and the liquid begins to thicken.

9. Transfer the filling to a bowl and refrigerate until cooled.

10. **To make the topping,** beat together the cream, confectioners' sugar, and vanilla until the mixture holds stiff peaks.

11. **To assemble the cake,** place one of the cake rounds, cut-side down, on a cake platter. Spoon the filling over the cake, spreading it in an even layer and letting the sauce soak into the cake. Top with a layer of whipped cream.

12. Place the second cake layer on top, cut-side down. Top with a layer of whipped cream.

13. Using a vegetable peeler, shave ribbons of chocolate from the bar onto a plate. Place the plate in the freezer for several minutes to firm up the shavings, then sprinkle them over the top of the cake. Garnish with the remaining cherries. Refrigerate until ready to serve.

SUBSTITUTION TIP: If you don't have cherry liqueur, you can substitute an equal quantity of cherry juice or water.

Bananas and Cream Icebox Cake

My family goes nuts for creamy banana desserts, like banana pudding and this easy-to-make classic icebox cake, which layers chocolate wafer cookies, thin slices of banana, and pillowy whipped cream. Because it seems like a throwback to simpler times (you know, when people had iceboxes), I created this sweet dessert for Grandparents' Day.

3 cups cold heavy (whipping) cream

½ cups confectioners' sugar

1 teaspoon vanilla extract

1 (9-ounce) package chocolate wafers

4 bananas, thinly sliced

3 ounces bittersweet baking chocolate

1. In a large bowl using an electric mixer or in the bowl of a stand mixer, combine the cream, confectioners' sugar, and vanilla and beat on medium-high speed until the mixture holds stiff peaks.

2. Spoon ¼ cup of the whipped cream into an 8-inch springform pan and spread it out in an even layer. Top with a layer of wafers and a layer of bananas. Repeat with whipped cream, wafers, and bananas until you have 4 layers of cookies. Finish with a layer of whipped cream.

3. Refrigerate for at least 4 hours or up to overnight.

4. Just before serving, use a vegetable peeler to shave the chocolate over the top. Carefully remove the sides of the springform pan and cut the cake into wedges to serve.

SUBSTITUTION TIP: You can substitute thin chocolate sandwich cookies for the wafers or use graham crackers, gingersnaps, or any other thin, crisp cookies you like.

Buttery Dinner Rolls

*E*very Thanksgiving table needs great dinner rolls, and these are irresistible. The recipe requires just a few ingredients, which you probably already have in your pantry, and 20 minutes of hands-on time. They turn out soft and fluffy, and you'll love how buttery they are. These rolls are a great addition to any holiday meal, but they're so easy that you'll probably find yourself making them all the time.

1 cup warm milk
(105°F to 110°F)

1 packet (2¼ teaspoons)
instant yeast

2 tablespoons granulated
sugar, divided

1 large egg

¼ cup unsalted butter, at
room temperature, cut into
pieces, plus 2 tablespoons
melted butter for brushing

1 teaspoon kosher salt

3 cups all-purpose
flour, plus more for
kneading (optional)

1 teaspoon cooking oil, plus
more for greasing the pan

1. In a large bowl using an electric mixer or in the bowl of a stand mixer, stir together the milk, yeast, and 1 tablespoon of sugar. Let stand for 5 to 10 minutes, until frothy.

2. Add the remaining tablespoon of sugar, the egg, ¼ cup of butter, the salt, and 1 cup of flour. Beat on low speed for about 30 seconds to moisten the flour, then add the remaining 2 cups of flour. Raise the mixer speed to medium and beat for about 2 minutes, until the mixture comes together in a sticky dough.

Beat for about 2 minutes more to knead the dough, or turn the dough out onto a lightly floured surface and knead by hand for about 4 minutes.

3. Lightly coat a large bowl with the oil and place the dough in it, turning to coat. Cover the bowl with a clean dish towel or plastic wrap, set it on your countertop, and let rise until doubled in in size, 1 to 2 hours.

4. Coat a 9-by-13-inch baking dish with oil or butter.

5. Punch down the risen dough and divide it in half. Then divide each half into 8 equal pieces. Roll each piece of dough into a ball. Arrange the balls in the prepared baking dish.
6. Cover the baking dish with a clean dish towel or plastic wrap and let rise in a warm place for about 1 hour, until the rolls puff up.
7. Preheat the oven to 350°F.
8. Bake the rolls until golden brown on top, about 25 minutes.
9. Remove the rolls from the oven and immediately brush the melted butter on top.
10. Serve warm or at room temperature.

TROUBLESHOOTING TIP: If your dough isn't rising, your kitchen may not be warm enough. You can try putting the dough in your oven with just the light on, which will be slightly warmer than your kitchen and draft-free.

Bacon Cheddar Biscuits

⇥ MAKES 12 BISCUITS ⇤

PREP TIME: 15 MINUTES • COOK TIME: 18 MINUTES

Woo-wee! Let me tell you about this one. Honestly, what could be better than flaky, buttery biscuits loaded with bacon and cheese? If you think making homemade biscuits sounds difficult, I promise this recipe will set you at ease. Follow the steps and get ready to enjoy an amazing treat. They're a great addition to Thanksgiving dinner or a breakfast or brunch spread.

3 cups all-purpose flour, plus additional for dusting

1 tablespoon baking powder

¾ teaspoon baking soda

1¼ teaspoons kosher salt

½ cup (1 stick) plus 1 tablespoon unsalted butter, cold, cut into small pieces

3 ounces shredded sharp cheddar cheese

5 bacon strips, cooked until crisp and then chopped

1 cup plus 2 tablespoons buttermilk

1. Preheat the oven to 450°F and line a large baking sheet with parchment paper.
2. In a large bowl, combine the flour, baking powder, baking soda, and salt.
3. Cut the butter into the flour mixture using a pastry cutter (or two knives) until the mixture resembles a coarse meal with pea-size lumps of butter.
4. Stir in the cheese and bacon. Add the buttermilk and stir gently until the mixture comes together in a soft dough.
5. Turn out the dough onto on a lightly floured surface and knead a few times. Using a lightly floured rolling pin, roll out the dough to about 1¼-inch thickness. Use a 2-inch round cutter to cut out 12 biscuits, then place them on the baking sheet.
6. Bake for 16 to 18 minutes, until golden brown and crisp.

ADVANCED TIP: Instead of cutting the butter into the flour with a pastry cutter, you can grate it using a box grater. Keep the butter whole and make sure it is very, very cold (ideally frozen solid) when you grate it. Use the large holes of the box grater to grate the butter into the flour.

Chapter 5

WINTER RECIPES

*Gingerbread
Cookies, page 100*

Gingerbread Cookies

❖ MAKES ABOUT 3 DOZEN COOKIES ❖

PREP TIME: 45 MINUTES, PLUS 20 MINUTES TO CHILL • COOK TIME: 10 MINUTES

*D*id you know gingerbread was popularized by none other than Queen Elizabeth I. Isn't that cool? This recipe is dear to my heart because it's the one my little sisters and I use every holiday season to make gingerbread people and houses. I am so happy to share our tradition with you so that you and your family can make it your own.

FOR THE COOKIES

½ cup (1 stick) plus 2 tablespoons unsalted butter, at room temperature

¾ cup dark brown sugar

½ cup molasses

1 large egg

1½ teaspoons vanilla extract

3 cups all-purpose flour

1 tablespoon ground ginger

2 teaspoons ground cinnamon

¼ teaspoon ground cloves

¾ teaspoon baking powder

½ teaspoon baking soda

½ teaspoon kosher salt

FOR THE ICING

3 cups confectioners' sugar

1½ tablespoons meringue powder

1 teaspoon cream of tartar

4 to 6 tablespoons water

½ teaspoon vanilla extract

Sprinkles (optional)

1. **To make the cookies,** preheat the oven to 350°F.
2. In a large bowl using an electric mixer or in the bowl of a stand mixer, cream together the butter, sugar, and molasses on medium-high speed until smooth and fluffy. Add the egg and vanilla and beat to incorporate.
3. In a medium bowl, whisk together the flour, ginger, cinnamon, cloves, baking powder, baking soda, and salt. Add the dry ingredients to the wet ingredients 1 cup at a time, beating after each addition to incorporate.
4. Divide the dough into two equal portions. Place each half between two sheets of parchment paper and roll out to ¼-inch thickness. Place the rolled-out dough on large baking sheets (just slide the parchment right onto the baking sheet) and chill in the refrigerator for 15 to 20 minutes.
5. Remove the dough from the refrigerator and slide the parchment onto a work surface. Cut out shapes using cookie cutters.

6. Arrange the cutouts on a parchment-lined baking sheet, leaving about 1 inch in between. Bake for 8 or 9 minutes, until the cookies are just set.

7. Remove the pan from the oven and let the cookies cool for a couple of minutes before transferring them from the pan to a wire rack to cool completely.

8. **To make the icing,** in a large bowl using an electric mixer or in the bowl of a stand mixer, combine the confectioners' sugar, meringue powder, and cream of tartar. Add 4 tablespoons of water and the vanilla and beat on low speed to combine. Add additional water as needed to achieve the right consistency. Raise the speed of the mixer gradually and beat until the icing is thick and glossy.

9. Transfer the icing to a piping bag fitted with a small round tip or to a resealable plastic bag with a corner snipped off to make a piping bag.

10. Decorate the cookies with the icing and add sprinkles as desired.

TECHNIQUE TIP: Meringue powder is a great alternative to raw egg whites to get the right consistency in your royal icing. You can find it in the baking aisle of many supermarkets or craft stores or online.

Hot Cocoa Cupcakes

⇥ MAKES 12 CUPCAKES ⇤

PREP TIME: **30 MINUTES** • COOK TIME: **18 MINUTES**

. . . .

*C*an you believe these decadent chocolate cupcakes topped with marshmallow buttercream taste exactly like a cup of hot cocoa in cake form? It's true! They've even got adorable candy cane cup handles to make them look just like little cups of steaming chocolate.

. . . .

FOR THE CUPCAKES

1 cup all-purpose flour

¾ cup unsweetened cocoa powder

1½ teaspoons baking powder

¼ teaspoon kosher salt

½ cup (1 stick) unsalted butter, at room temperature

1 cup granulated sugar

2 large eggs

2 teaspoons vanilla extract

½ cup heavy (whipping) cream

FOR THE FROSTING

6 tablespoons unsalted butter, at room temperature

½ cup marshmallow creme

½ cup confectioners' sugar

½ teaspoon vanilla extract

FOR DECORATING

36 mini marshmallows

12 mini candy canes

. . . .

1. **To make the cupcakes,** preheat the oven to 350°F and line a 12-cup muffin tin with paper cupcake liners.
2. In a medium bowl, whisk together the flour, cocoa, baking powder, and salt.
3. In a large bowl using an electric mixer or in the bowl of a stand mixer, cream together the butter and sugar on medium-high speed until light and fluffy. Add the eggs and vanilla and beat to incorporate. Add the cream and beat to incorporate.
4. Transfer the batter to the prepared muffin tin, filling each cup about two-thirds full. Bake for about 18 minutes, until a toothpick inserted in the center comes out clean.
5. Remove the pan from the oven and let the cupcakes cool for a few minutes before transferring them to a wire rack to cool completely.
6. **To make the frosting,** in a medium bowl using an electric mixer or in the bowl of a stand mixer, beat the butter on medium speed until creamy and smooth. Add the marshmallow creme and beat to incorporate. Add the confectioners' sugar and beat until the mixture is smooth and thick. Add the vanilla and beat to incorporate.

7. Transfer the frosting to a piping bag fitted with a round or open star tip or to a resealable plastic bag with a corner snipped off to make a piping bag.

8. Once the cupcakes are completely cooled, pipe the frosting on top in a spiral starting at the outer edge and working toward the middle.

9. **To decorate the cupcakes,** top each cupcake with 3 mini marshmallows.

10. To make candy cane mug handles, use a sharp knife or scissors to cut the hooks off the candy canes, cutting at an angle so that the bottom of the hook lies against the side of the cupcake. Place the hooks on the edges of the cupcakes, tucking the top into the frosting so that it looks like a handle on a mug. (The cupcake liner is the mug.)

11. Take the extra bits of candy cane that you trimmed off and place them in a resealable bag. Use a rolling pin or meat tenderizer to crush the candy. Sprinkle the crushed candy cane over the frosting on the cupcakes.

SUBSTITUTION TIP: Instead of marshmallow buttercream, you can top the cupcakes with regular whipped cream or vanilla buttercream.

White Chocolate Sparkle Cake

❧ SERVES 12 ❧

PREP TIME: 40 MINUTES, PLUS 1 HOUR TO CHILL • COOK TIME: 30 MINUTES

*T*his is the ideal dessert for ringing in the new year. It's got double white chocolate—in the cake and the frosting—so the flavor is to die for. And the sparkles! So pretty that this cake is like a celebration of itself.

FOR THE CAKE

Butter and flour, for preparing the pans

8 ounces white chocolate, chopped

¾ cup hot water

3¾ cups all-purpose flour

2¼ cups granulated sugar

1 teaspoon baking powder

2 teaspoons baking soda

1 teaspoon kosher salt

1½ cups (3 sticks) unsalted butter, at room temperature

4 large eggs

1 cup sour cream

FOR THE FROSTING

¼ cup heavy (whipping) cream

12 ounces white chocolate, chopped

2 cups unsalted butter, at room temperature

4 cups confectioners' sugar

1 teaspoon vanilla

FOR DECORATING

Silver or gold sanding sugar

1. **To make the cake,** preheat the oven to 350°F and butter and flour three (8-inch) round cake pans.

2. Place the white chocolate in a medium bowl and pour the hot water over it. Let stand for a few minutes and then stir until the chocolate is completely melted and the mixture is smooth.

3. In a separate medium bowl, whisk together the flour, sugar, baking powder, baking soda, and salt.

4. In a large bowl using an electric mixer or in the bowl of a stand mixer, beat the butter on medium-high speed until smooth and fluffy. Add the eggs and sour cream, beating to mix.

5. Add the dry ingredients to the wet ingredients in a few batches and beat after each addition to incorporate. Add the white chocolate mixture and beat to combine well.

6. Divide the mixture evenly among the prepared baking pans. Bake for about 30 minutes, until the top springs back when pressed.

7. Remove the cakes from the oven and set on a wire rack to cool completely.

8. **To make the frosting,** place the cream and white chocolate in a microwave-safe bowl and heat in 30-second intervals, stirring in between, until the chocolate is

completely melted and the mixture is smooth. Set aside to cool.

9. In a large bowl using an electric mixer or in the bowl of a stand mixer, beat the butter on medium-high speed until smooth and fluffy. Add the confectioners' sugar 1 cup at a time, beating after each addition. Beat in the vanilla.

10. With the mixer running, drizzle in the white chocolate and cream mixture. Beat until the frosting is a thick, spreadable consistency.

11. **To assemble the cake,** once the cakes are completely cooled, run a knife around the outside edge of each and invert them onto a work surface. Trim the tops if necessary to make them flat.

12. Place the bottom layer of the cake, cut-side down, on a cake plate or platter. Spread buttercream over the top in an even layer. Place the second cake layer on top, cut-side down, and spread another layer of buttercream on top. Repeat with the final layer of cake.

13. Crumb coat the cake by spreading a thin layer of buttercream around the sides of the cake, completely covering it. Refrigerate the cake for about 30 minutes to give the buttercream a chance to set up.

14. Spread the remaining buttercream around the sides and top of the cake, covering them completely, and smooth the sides with an offset spatula or other tool. Return the cake to the refrigerator to chill for another 30 minutes.

15. Coat the sides and top of the cake generously with sanding sugar, pressing the sugar into the frosting to help it stick.

ADVANCED TIP: If you have extra buttercream, put it in a piping bag fitted with a star tip and pipe several flowers onto parchment paper. Transfer to the freezer and freeze for at least 30 minutes. Once the flowers are frozen, transfer them to the top of the cake.

Pink Champagne Cupcakes

❖ MAKES 24 CUPCAKES ❖

PREP TIME: **20 MINUTES** • COOK TIME: **20 MINUTES**

*T*here's nothing like a glass of pink Champagne to tickle your fancy. Well, nothing except these fun and festive Pink Champagne Cupcakes, which add a bit of cuteness and class to your holiday celebrations.

FOR THE CUPCAKES

3 cups all-purpose flour

1 tablespoon baking powder

½ teaspoon kosher salt

1 cup (2 sticks) unsalted butter, at room temperature

2 cups granulated sugar

4 large eggs

1 tablespoon vanilla extract

1 cup Champagne

Red gel food coloring

FOR THE FROSTING

½ cup unsalted butter, at room temperature

4 cups confectioners' sugar

¼ cup Champagne

1 teaspoon vanilla extract

Red gel food coloring

FOR DECORATING

Pink sanding sugar

Pink pearl sprinkles

1. **To make the cupcakes,** preheat the oven to 350°F and line two (12-cup) muffin tins with paper cupcake liners.
2. In a medium bowl, combine the flour, baking powder, and salt.
3. In a large bowl using an electric mixer or in the bowl of a stand mixer, cream together the butter and sugar on medium-high speed until pale yellow and fluffy. Add the eggs one at a time, beating until incorporated. Add the vanilla and beat until incorporated.
4. Add half the dry ingredients to the wet ingredients and beat on medium speed until incorporated. Add the Champagne and beat until incorporated. Add the remaining flour mixture and beat just until incorporated. Add 3 to 5 drops of gel food coloring and beat to incorporate. Start with 3 drops and add additional as needed to achieve the color you want.
5. Scoop the batter into the prepared muffin tin, filling each liner about two-thirds full. Bake for 18 to 20 minutes, until a toothpick inserted in the center comes out clean. Let cool in the pan for a minute or two, then transfer to a wire rack to cool completely.

CONTINUED >>

6. **To make the frosting,** in a large bowl using an electric mixer or in the bowl of a stand mixer, beat the butter until smooth and fluffy. Add the confectioners' sugar 1 cup at a time, beating after each addition. Beat in the Champagne and vanilla, then add 3 to 5 drops of gel food coloring, starting with 3 drops and adding additional as needed to achieve the desired color.

7. **To decorate the cupcakes,** transfer the buttercream to a piping bag fitted with a star tip or to a resealable plastic bag with one corner snipped off to make a piping bag. Pipe the frosting onto the cupcakes in a spiral pattern, starting at the outside edge and working your way in and up until you get to the center. When you get to the center, stop applying pressure to the piping bag and lift straight up to complete the spiral.

8. Finish the cupcakes by dusting the tops with sanding sugar and scattering on the pearl sprinkles.

SUBSTITUTION TIP: You don't need to use an expensive Champagne in this recipe. Any sparkling wine will do. In fact, even a still white wine will provide the touch of flavor you want here.

Conversation Hearts Cookies

↯ MAKES ABOUT 2 DOZEN COOKIES (DEPENDING
ON THE SIZE OF YOUR CUTTER) ↯

PREP TIME: 40 MINUTES, PLUS 1 HOUR TO CHILL AND OVERNIGHT TO SET

COOK TIME: 12 MINUTES

Remember those little heart candies that had cute sayings on them but tasted like chalk? These cookies keep the messaging, but they taste great. Add classic messages or make up your own. Here are some fun options: Love U, Choose Me, You're Hot, Be Mine, XOXO, Cutie Pie, or I'll Drive!

FOR THE COOKIES

3 cups all-purpose flour

¾ teaspoon baking powder

¼ teaspoon kosher salt

1 cup unsalted butter, at room temperature

1 cup granulated sugar

1 large egg

1 tablespoon milk

1 teaspoon vanilla extract

FOR THE ICING

3 cups confectioners' sugar

1½ tablespoons meringue powder

4 to 6 tablespoons water

½ teaspoon vanilla extract

Gel food coloring in various colors (pink/red, green, blue, yellow)

Red food marker

1. **To make the cookies,** in a medium bowl, whisk together the flour, baking powder, and salt.

2. In a large bowl using an electric mixer or in the bowl of a stand mixer, cream together the butter and sugar on medium-high speed until pale yellow and fluffy. Add the egg, milk, and vanilla and beat to combine.

3. With the mixer running on low speed, gradually add the dry ingredients, beating until the mixture is well combined and begins to pull away from the sides of the bowl. Divide the dough into two equal portions.

4. Roll out one of the dough portions between two pieces of parchment paper to ¼-inch thickness. Remove the top piece of parchment and slide the remaining piece of parchment onto a baking sheet. Using a heart-shaped cutter, cut out as many cookies as you can. Carefully remove the excess cookie dough from around the cutouts. (You can reroll this and use it to make more cookies.) Cover the pan with plastic wrap and chill for 1 hour.

CONTINUED >>

5. Preheat the oven to 350°F.

6. Bake the cookies for 10 to 12 minutes, until the edges are just starting to brown a bit. Transfer to a wire rack to cool completely.

7. **To make the icing,** in a large bowl using an electric mixer or in the bowl of a stand mixer, combine the confectioners' sugar and meringue powder. Add 4 tablespoons of water and the vanilla and beat on low speed to combine. Add additional water as needed to achieve the right consistency. The icing should be fairly thick and very smooth. Raise the speed of the mixer gradually and beat until the icing is thick and glossy.

8. Divide the icing among as many bowls as you need for your different colors. Mix a few drops of food coloring into each bowl to achieve your desired shade, keeping in mind that the color will darken a bit as the icing dries.

9. Fill a piping bag fitted with a small, round tip half full with one color of icing. Pipe a thin outline of icing around the outside edge of some of the cookies. (Divide the total number of cookies by however many colors of icing you have.)

10. Transfer any remaining icing in that color back to the bowl with that color of icing. Add about a teaspoon of water to the icing to thin it, stirring to mix well. Add additional water as needed to get it to the consistency of a thick syrup. Return the icing to the piping bag and use it to "flood" the top of the cookie inside the icing outline. You can use a toothpick to spread the icing into any missed spots.

11. Repeat this with all the colors of icing and all the cookies. Once all the cookies are iced, let them sit out at room temperature, uncovered, overnight. The icing will dry and harden.

12. Once the icing is completely dry, use the food marker to write words or phrases on the cookies. Add a few silly ones, too!

ADVANCED TIP: If you are good with a piping bag, you can make a small batch of red royal icing and pipe the words onto the cookies using a small, round piping tip instead of the food marker.

New York Cheesecake

❖ SERVES 10 ❖

PREP TIME: 30 MINUTES, PLUS 12 HOURS TO CHILL

COOK TIME: 1 HOUR 20 MINUTES, PLUS 1 HOUR MORE IN THE TURNED-OFF OVEN

I lived in New York for about eight years, and this is my version of the classic cheesecake that I fell in love with way back at the iconic NYC restaurant Junior's. New York cheesecake is unique because instead of being cooked in a water bath, it is cooked at a high temperature for a brief period and then slow-cooked at a low temperature. The result is a rich, creamy cheesecake with a lightly browned exterior.

FOR THE CRUST

Nonstick cooking spray, for greasing the pan

1½ cups graham cracker crumbs (from 12 whole cracker sheets)

5 tablespoons unsalted butter, melted

2 tablespoons granulated sugar

Pinch kosher salt

FOR THE FILLING

32 ounces cream cheese, at room temperature

1¾ cups granulated sugar

3 tablespoons all-purpose flour

4 large eggs, at room temperature

2 large egg yolks, at room temperature

½ cup heavy (whipping) cream

1 tablespoon vanilla extract

Grated zest of 1 lemon

¼ teaspoon kosher salt

FOR THE SAUCE

1 pound fresh strawberries, sliced

⅓ cup granulated sugar

1 tablespoon freshly squeezed lemon juice

1. **To make the crust,** preheat the oven to 375°F and wrap a 9-inch springform pan with two layers of heavy-duty aluminum foil so that the entire bottom and outside of the pan is covered to insulate the contents and prevent the batter from leaking out. Coat the inside of the pan with cooking spray.

2. In a medium bowl, stir together the graham cracker crumbs, butter, sugar, and salt until fully moistened. Transfer the mixture to the prepared springform pan and press it into an even layer covering the bottom of the pan.

3. Bake for 10 minutes, remove the pan from the oven, and raise the oven temperature to 475°F.

4. **To make the filling,** in a large bowl using an electric mixer or in the bowl of a stand mixer, beat the cream cheese on medium speed until smooth, about 2 minutes. Add the sugar and beat to combine well.

5. Add the flour and beat to incorporate. Add the eggs and egg yolks and beat to incorporate. Add the cream, vanilla, lemon zest, and salt and beat just until the mixture is smooth and well combined. Transfer the batter to the pan with the parbaked crust.

6. Bake for 10 minutes, then reduce the oven temperature to 225°F. Bake for 1 hour, until the edges begin to turn golden brown and the cake is set around the edges but still a bit loose in the center.

7. Turn off the oven, open the door halfway, and leave the cake inside for 1 hour more.

8. Remove the cake from the oven and set it on a wire rack to cool to room temperature. Cover and refrigerate for at least 12 hours.

9. **To make the sauce,** in a medium saucepan over medium heat, stir together the strawberries, sugar, and lemon juice and bring to a boil. Reduce the heat to low and simmer, stirring occasionally, for about 20 minutes, until the strawberries break down and the sauce thickens. Remove from the heat and set aside to cool to room temperature.

10. To serve, carefully remove the sides of the springform pan from the cake. Spoon the sauce over the cake, then cut the cake into wedges and serve immediately. Alternatively, you can spoon the sauce onto each slice just before serving.

MAKE AHEAD TIP: You can make this cheesecake ahead of time and store it in the refrigerator for up to 2 days or in the freezer for up to 3 months. To freeze, wrap the chilled cake well in two layers of plastic wrap. For extra protection, place the wrapped cake in a resealable plastic bag. Let the cake thaw overnight in the refrigerator before serving.

Frosted Football Brownies

*C*elebrate football season with these from-scratch, football-shaped brownies topped with a rich chocolate ganache. They're a guaranteed touchdown.

FOR THE BROWNIES

Nonstick cooking spray, for greasing the pan

4 large eggs

1 cup granulated sugar

1 cup brown sugar

8 ounces unsalted butter, melted

1¼ cups unsweetened cocoa powder

2 teaspoons vanilla extract

½ cup all-purpose flour

¼ teaspoon kosher salt

FOR THE GANACHE

1 cup semisweet chocolate chips

½ cup heavy (whipping) cream

1 tablespoon unsalted butter, at room temperature

1 teaspoon vanilla extract

Pinch kosher salt

FOR DECORATING

White writing icing

1. **To make the brownies,** preheat the oven to 300°F and coat an 8-inch square baking pan generously with cooking spray.

2. In a large bowl using an electric mixer or in the bowl of a stand mixer, beat the eggs on medium-high speed for 2 to 3 minutes, until frothy. Add the granulated sugar, brown sugar, butter, cocoa, vanilla, flour, and salt and beat until smooth.

3. Transfer the batter to the prepared baking pan and bake for about 45 minutes, until a toothpick inserted in the center comes out clean. Remove the pan from the oven and set it on a wire rack to cool to room temperature.

4. **To make the ganache,** put the chocolate chips, cream, and butter in a microwave-safe bowl and heat on 50 percent power in 30-second intervals, stirring in between, until the

chocolate is completely melted and the mixture is smooth. Stir in the vanilla and salt. Let stand for about 5 minutes to cool a bit and then pour the mixture over the brownies in the pan.

5. Refrigerate for at least 30 minutes to allow the frosting to set.

6. Using a knife or a football-shaped cutter, cut the brownies into footballs, then use the writing icing to draw stitches on the footballs. Serve the brownies at room temperature.

ADVANCED TIP: Take the flavors up a notch by reducing the heavy cream in the ganache recipe to ¼ cup plus 2 tablespoons and then stirring in 2 tablespoons of Irish cream liqueur along with the vanilla and salt.

Candy Cane Chocolate Bundt Cake

✤ SERVES 10 ✤

PREP TIME: **20 MINUTES** • COOK TIME: **55 MINUTES**

I love Bundt cakes because they come out of the pan looking stunning without any embellishment. This is a moist, peppermint-chocolate cake topped with a glaze of chocolate ganache and crushed candy canes. It's an easy-yet-impressive dessert for any holiday party.

FOR THE CAKE

Butter and flour or cooking spray, for preparing the pan

1¾ cups all-purpose flour

2 cups granulated sugar

¾ cup unsweetened cocoa powder

1 teaspoon baking powder

2 teaspoons baking soda

1 teaspoon kosher salt

½ cup vegetable oil

½ cup heavy (whipping) cream or sour cream

2 large eggs

1½ teaspoons peppermint extract

1 teaspoon vanilla extract

1 cup strong brewed coffee

FOR THE GANACHE AND DECORATING

¾ cup heavy (whipping) cream

5 ounces dark chocolate, chopped

1 teaspoon vanilla extract

½ cup crushed candy canes

1. **To make the cake,** preheat the oven to 350°F. Lightly coat a Bundt pan with butter and flour or coat it with cooking spray.
2. In a large bowl using an electric mixer or in the bowl of a stand mixer, combine the flour, sugar, cocoa, baking powder, baking soda, and salt and mix to combine.
3. In a medium bowl, whisk together the oil, cream, eggs, peppermint extract, and vanilla. Add the wet ingredients to the dry ingredients and beat on low speed to combine. Add the coffee and beat just to incorporate.
4. Transfer the batter to the prepared pan and bake for about 55 minutes, until a toothpick inserted in the center comes out clean.
5. Remove the pan from the oven and place it on a wire rack to cool. Once the cake has cooled significantly, invert it onto a cake platter and let cool to room temperature.

6. **To make the ganache,** in a small saucepan, heat the cream until it is almost boiling. Put the chocolate in a heat-safe bowl and pour the hot cream over the top. Let stand for about 1 minute, then stir until the chocolate is completely melted and the mixture is smooth. Stir in the vanilla extract.

7. Pour the ganache over the top of the cake, letting it run down the sides. Sprinkle the crushed candy canes on top. Serve the cake at room temperature.

TECHNIQUE TIP: You can make the ganache in the microwave if you prefer. Combine the chocolate and cream in a glass measuring cup with a spout and heat it in the microwave on 50 percent power in 30-second intervals, stirring in between, until the chocolate is completely melted and the mixture is smooth. Drizzle the mixture over the cake once the cake has cooled.

Cheesecake Holiday Bars

⤙ MAKES 15 TREES ⤚

PREP TIME: 30 MINUTES, PLUS 3 HOURS TO CHILL • COOK TIME: 40 MINUTES

*T*hese creamy cheesecake triangles are dipped in white chocolate and decorated in any holiday colors you choose! They're fun to make, fun to eat, and a festive way to deck your dessert table.

FOR THE CHEESECAKE

Nonstick cooking spray, for greasing the pan

1 cup chocolate wafer crumbs

¼ cup unsalted butter, melted

16 ounces cream cheese, at room temperature

½ cup granulated sugar

¼ cup sour cream

2 large eggs

1 teaspoon vanilla

FOR THE COATING

3½ cups white chocolate chips

3 tablespoons shortening

Gel food coloring

White or black writing icing

Sprinkles or nonpareils

1. **To make the cheesecake bars,** preheat the oven to 300°F and line an 8-inch square baking pan with heavy-duty aluminum foil, extending the foil over the sides of the pan like a sling. Coat the foil with cooking spray. Also line a baking sheet with parchment paper.

2. In small bowl, mix together the wafer crumbs and butter until the crumbs are thoroughly moistened. Press the crumb mixture into the bottom of the prepared pan.

3. In a large bowl using an electric mixer or in the bowl of a stand mixer, beat together the cream cheese and sugar on medium speed until smooth and fluffy. Add the sour cream, eggs, and vanilla and beat to incorporate.

4. Pour the filling mixture over the crust. Bake for 30 to 40 minutes, until the cheesecake is set around the edges but still a bit wobbly in the center.

5. Remove the pan from the oven and set it on a wire rack to cool for 20 to 30 minutes before covering with plastic wrap and chilling in the freezer for 2 hours.

6. Lift the cheesecake out of the pan using the foil sling. Using a sharp knife, cut the cheesecake into 3 strips. Then cut each strip into 5 bars. Place each on the parchment-lined baking sheet. Freeze the trees for 30 minutes.

7. **To make the coating,** combine the white chocolate chips and shortening in a microwave-safe bowl and heat on 50 percent power in 30-second intervals, stirring in between, until the chocolate is completely melted and the mixture is smooth. Stir in 3 drops of your favorite holiday color food coloring.

8. Using toothpicks to hold the bars, dip each one into the chocolate mixture to fully coat it and then let the excess drip back into the bowl. Return the dipped trees to the parchment-lined baking sheet. Freeze for 30 minutes.

9. Use the writing icing to pipe decorations on the bars and then add the sprinkles.

ADVANCED TIP: You can use sugar pearls as decorations, too. Add them right after dipping the bars, before the chocolate has hardened.

Peppermint Macarons with White Chocolate Buttercream

✦ MAKES 12 MACARONS ✦

PREP TIME: 30 MINUTES, PLUS 30 MINUTES TO DRY • COOK TIME: 20 MINUTES

. . . .

Holy macarons! It's that magical time of year between Thanksgiving and Christmas when the flavor of peppermint takes over the world. Macarons may seem intimidating, but these are gorgeous, taste amazing, and really aren't that hard to make. Once you master the process, you'll be the hit of every party.

. . . .

FOR THE MACARONS

1 cup almond flour

⅔ cup confectioners' sugar

2 medium egg whites, at room temperature

Pinch kosher salt

¼ cup granulated sugar

⅛ teaspoon peppermint extract

Red gel food coloring (optional)

FOR THE FROSTING

¼ cup white chocolate chips

½ cup unsalted butter, at room temperature

1 cup confectioners' sugar

1 teaspoon vanilla extract

Pinch kosher salt

. . . .

1. **To make the macarons,** preheat the oven to 300°F and line a large baking sheet with parchment paper.

2. Sift the almond flour and confectioners' sugar into a large bowl. Discard any lumps.

3. In a separate large bowl using an electric mixer with a whisk attachment or in the bowl of a stand mixer with a whisk attachment, combine the egg whites and salt until soft peaks form. While whisking, add the granulated sugar a little at a time. Continue to whisk until the egg whites are glossy and thick enough that you could hold the bowl upside down without the mixture falling out.

4. Gently fold the confectioners' sugar and almond flour mixture, the peppermint extract, and 3 drops of food coloring (if using) into the whipped egg whites.

5. Transfer the mixture to a piping bag fitted with a 1-centimeter round tip.

6. Pipe 12 (1-inch) dollops of batter onto the parchment-lined baking sheet, spacing them about 1½ inches apart.

7. Tap the baking sheet on the countertop two or three times to pop any air bubbles that have formed in the batter and then let stand at room temperature for

CONTINUED >>

about 30 minutes to dry out the surface of the batter.

8. Bake for 18 to 20 minutes, until the cookies have risen a bit and feel firm, opening the oven door about halfway through cooking to release any steam that has built up and then closing it again.

9. Slide the parchment paper onto a wire rack and let the cookies cool completely on the parchment.

10. **To make the frosting,** melt the white chocolate chips in the top of a double boiler.

11. In a medium bowl using an electric mixer or in the bowl of a stand mixer, beat the butter on medium speed until fluffy and pale yellow. Add the white chocolate and mix to combine.

12. Add the confectioners' sugar, vanilla, and salt and beat on low until incorporated. Raise the speed to high and beat for about 3 minutes, until the mixture is thick and fluffy.

13. Spoon or pipe a dollop of buttercream onto the flat side of half the macarons. Sandwich together the unfrosted and frosted cookies.

14. For best results, refrigerate the macarons for 24 hours before serving.

TECHNIQUE TIP: You can buy a special silicon baking mat for making macarons. It has a template printed right on it to help you get evenly sized cookies. You can also make your own by tracing the bottom of a small juice glass or another round object onto parchment paper.

Molten Lava Cakes

✦ MAKES 4 CAKES ✦

PREP TIME: **10 MINUTES** • COOK TIME: **12 MINUTES**

. . . .

*T*his is one of my absolute favorite recipes. Make it for that special someone for Valentine's Day. If you really want them to fall hard, be sure to serve it warm with a scoop of vanilla ice cream on top.

. . . .

Butter and unsweetened cocoa powder, for preparing the ramekins

½ cup (1 stick) unsalted butter

6 ounces dark chocolate, chopped

2 large eggs

2 large egg yolks

¼ cup granulated sugar

Pinch kosher salt

2 tablespoons all-purpose flour

. . . .

1. Preheat the oven to 450°F. Coat four (6-ounce) ramekins with butter and dust them with cocoa powder.

2. Put the butter and chocolate in the top of a double boiler and heat over simmering water until the chocolate is completely melted and the mixture is smooth. (Alternatively, you can combine the butter and chocolate in a microwave-safe bowl and heat on 50 percent power in 30-second intervals, stirring in between.)

3. In a medium bowl using an electric mixer or in the bowl of a stand mixer, beat the eggs and egg yolks with the sugar and salt on high speed until thick and pale yellow.

4. Gently fold the chocolate into the egg and sugar mixture. Fold in the flour until well incorporated. Transfer the batter to the ramekins, dividing it equally.

5. Set the filled ramekins on a baking sheet and bake for about 12 minutes, until the cakes are firm around the edges but the centers are not quite set. Remove from the oven and let cool for a minute or two. Run a knife around the edge of each cake and invert it onto a serving plate. Serve immediately.

MAKE AHEAD TIP: These cakes really need to be served warm out of the oven for the full, oozy effect. You can make the batter and fill the ramekins ahead of time. The ramekins can be refrigerated, covered with plastic wrap, for a day or two. To finish, allow the batter to come to room temperature and then bake as directed.

Eggnog Bundt Cake

⇥ SERVES 10 ⇤

PREP TIME: **15 MINUTES** • COOK TIME: **45 MINUTES**

- -

*T*his Bundt cake recipe with a sugar glaze is deliciously seasonal, with rich, boozy eggnog flavor baked in. I love to serve this at holiday parties, with or without a pitcher of eggnog on the side. Feel free to leave out the rum if you like, but it does add a nice little kick.

- -

FOR THE CAKE

Butter and flour or nonstick cooking spray, for preparing the pan

2 cups all-purpose flour

1 teaspoon baking powder

½ teaspoon baking soda

½ teaspoon ground cinnamon

¼ teaspoon kosher salt

⅛ teaspoon ground nutmeg

½ cup unsalted butter, at room temperature

½ cup granulated sugar

½ cup brown sugar

2 large eggs

2 tablespoons rum (optional)

1 teaspoon vanilla extract

1 cup eggnog

FOR THE GLAZE

1 cup confectioners' sugar

¼ cup eggnog

¼ teaspoon ground cinnamon

Pinch kosher salt

- -

1. **To make the cake,** preheat the oven to 350°F and lightly coat a Bundt pan with butter and flour or coat it with cooking spray.

2. In a medium bowl, whisk together the flour, baking powder, baking soda, cinnamon, salt, and nutmeg.

3. In a large bowl using an electric mixer or in the bowl of a stand mixer, cream together the butter and both sugars on medium-high speed until light and fluffy. Add the eggs one at a time, beating to incorporate after each addition. Add the rum (if using), and vanilla and beat to incorporate.

4. Add half of the dry ingredients to the wet ingredients and beat to incorporate. Add the eggnog and beat to mix well. Finally, add the remaining dry mixture and beat until

it is incorporated and the mixture is smooth.

5. Transfer the batter to the prepared pan and bake for about 45 minutes, until a toothpick inserted in the center comes out clean. Remove the cake from the oven and let it cool in the pan for 10 to 15 minutes before inverting it onto a platter.

6. **To make the glaze,** in a small bowl, stir together the confectioners' sugar, eggnog, cinnamon, and salt until smooth. Drizzle the glaze over the cake while it is still warm.

TROUBLESHOOTING TIP: Bundt pans tend to have a lot of nooks and crannies where batter can stick. Be sure to coat the inside of the pan very well with either butter and a dusting of flour or a generous coating of cooking spray to ensure that your cake comes out easily.

Salted Caramel Pecan Tart

⤳ SERVES 10 ⤶

PREP TIME: 20 MINUTES, PLUS 1 HOUR TO CHILL · COOK TIME: 50 MINUTES

. . . .

*O*nce the winter season settles in, all I want to do is bake. When the weather turns cold, the first thing I do is throw on my apron, heat up my oven, and get out the sugar and flour. This rich caramel tart with toasted pecans and a buttery crust is always one of the first things on my baking list.

. . . .

FOR THE CRUST

1¼ cups all-purpose flour

½ cup confectioners' sugar

⅛ teaspoon kosher salt

½ cup (1 stick) unsalted butter, cold

1 large egg

½ teaspoon vanilla extract

FOR THE FILLING

1 cup brown sugar

½ cup heavy (whipping) cream

½ cup (1 stick) unsalted butter, cut into small pieces

⅛ teaspoon kosher salt

2 teaspoons vanilla extract

2 cups coarsely chopped pecans, toasted

Flaky sea salt (such as fleur de sel)

. . . .

1. **To make the crust,** in a food processor or in a medium bowl, combine the flour, confectioners' sugar, and salt. Add the butter and pulse in the food processor or cut in with a pastry cutter until the mixture resembles a coarse meal with butter clumps the size of peas.

2. Add the egg and vanilla and process or mix until the dough comes together in a ball. Form the ball into a disk, wrap it tightly in plastic wrap, and refrigerate for 1 hour.

3. Preheat the oven to 350°F.

4. Once the dough has chilled, roll it out to between ⅛-inch and ¼-inch thickness and press it into an 11-inch tart pan with a removable bottom. Trim off the excess hanging over the sides. Poke several holes in the bottom of the crust with a fork. Place a piece of parchment paper over the crust and fill with pie weights or dried beans. Bake for 20 minutes. Remove from the oven and remove the pie weights and parchment.

5. **To make the filling,** in a medium saucepan set over medium-high heat, combine the sugar, cream, butter, salt, and vanilla and bring to a boil. Remove the pan from the heat and stir in the pecans.

6. Transfer the filling to the crust. Bake until the crust is golden brown and the filling is bubbling, 25 to 30 minutes.

7. Remove the pan from the oven and sprinkle flaky sea salt on top. Set the pan on a wire rack and let the tart cool completely before serving.

TECHNIQUE TIP: To toast pecans, preheat the oven to 350°F and line a rimmed baking sheet with parchment paper. Spread the nuts in a single layer on the prepared pan and toast for 8 to 10 minutes, stirring once or twice, until nicely browned.

New Year's Morning Strata

✢ SERVES 4 TO 6 ✢

PREP TIME: 10 MINUTES, PLUS OVERNIGHT TO CHILL • COOK TIME: 50 MINUTES

A strata is a breakfast casserole that is similar to a savory bread pudding. It's perfect for New Year's morning because you can prepare it the day before, store it in the refrigerator, and bake it as soon as you roll out of bed at the crack of noon. This one has spinach, ham, and Gruyère cheese, but you can mix it up with different meats, vegetables, and cheeses if you like.

Butter or nonstick cooking spray, for greasing the pan

2½ cups (1-inch) pieces of stale bread

6 large eggs

2 cups milk

½ teaspoon kosher salt

½ teaspoon freshly ground black pepper

Pinch ground nutmeg

1 cup diced cooked ham

1 (10-ounce) package frozen spinach, thawed, squeezed dry, and chopped

1 cup shredded Gruyère cheese, divided

1. Lightly butter a 1½-quart baking dish or coat with cooking spray.

2. Spread the bread cubes in an even layer in the prepared baking dish.

3. In a medium bowl, whisk together the eggs, milk, salt, pepper, and nutmeg. Stir in the ham, spinach, and ½ cup of cheese.

4. Pour the egg mixture into the prepared baking dish, tossing to make sure all the bread is coated. Sprinkle the remaining ½ cup of cheese over the top.

5. Cover the pan with aluminum foil and refrigerate overnight.

6. Preheat the oven to 350°F and let the strata come to room temperature.

7. Bake, covered, for 35 minutes. Remove the foil and bake for about 15 minutes more, until the strata puffs up, the edges are nicely browned, and the center is set. Remove from the oven and let cool for about 10 minutes before serving.

SUBSTITUTION TIP: Strata is endlessly variable. You can substitute cooked bacon for the ham and chard or kale for the spinach. Or use blanched asparagus or broccoli florets. Add halved cherry tomatoes, sautéed mushrooms, or sliced scallions.

Spinach-Parmesan Puff Pastry Christmas Tree

✦ SERVES 6 ✦

PREP TIME: **30 MINUTES** • COOK TIME: **15 MINUTES**

This holiday appetizer uses frozen puff pastry and is much easier to create than you would think from how stunning it is. Serve it with glasses of crisp bubbly as a pre-dinner nosh or as part of a holiday appetizer spread.

1 garlic clove

1 cup frozen chopped spinach, thawed and squeezed dry

⅓ cup mayonnaise

¼ cup cream cheese

⅓ cup freshly grated Parmesan cheese, plus 2 tablespoons

¼ teaspoon kosher salt

¼ teaspoon freshly ground black pepper

1 (17.3-ounce) package frozen puff pastry (2 sheets), thawed

1 large egg whisked with 1 tablespoon water

2 tablespoons minced fresh flat-leaf parsley

1. Preheat the oven to 375°F.
2. In a food processor, mince the garlic. Add the spinach, mayonnaise, cream cheese, ⅓ cup of Parmesan cheese, salt, and pepper and pulse until the ingredients are well combined. (If you don't have a food processor, you can mince the garlic and mix all of the ingredients by hand or with an electric mixer.)
3. Lightly flour a sheet of parchment paper and lay one of the sheets of pastry on top. Use a rolling pin to roll it out to a rectangle about 13-by-11-inches. Transfer the parchment paper with the pastry to a large baking sheet.
4. Spread the spinach mixture evenly over the pastry, leaving a ½-inch border around the edge.
5. Roll out the second sheet of puff pastry to a 13-by-11-inch rectangle and place it on top of the first. Press gently around the edges to seal the two pastry sheets together.
6. Cut out a Christmas tree–shaped triangle from a sheet of paper or a piece of cardboard to use as a template. Place the template on top of the pastry and use a sharp knife to cut the pastry to match the shape (reserve the cut-off pieces).

CONTINUED >>

7. To make the branches of the tree, cut slits into the sides of the tree, leaving about 1½ inches in the center uncut (this will be the tree's trunk). Make several corresponding cuts down each side of the tree.

8. With the tree perpendicular to your body, start at the bottom and twist each branch away from you and then press the end of each branch to secure it to the parchment so that it doesn't unwind itself.

9. You can cut the extra pieces of pastry into stars or other shapes for decorating the tree or the serving platter.

Arrange them around the tree on the baking sheet.

10. Use a pastry brush to coat the tree and any extra shapes with the egg wash. Sprinkle the remaining 2 tablespoons of Parmesan cheese over the top.

11. Bake until the pastry has puffed up and turned golden brown, 12 to 15 minutes.

12. Remove from the oven and carefully slide the pastry onto a serving platter. Sprinkle the parsley over the top and serve immediately.

ADVANCED TIP: For an even more festive look, you can decorate the tree with small pieces of red and green bell pepper or grape tomatoes cut in half. Add the vegetables before baking.

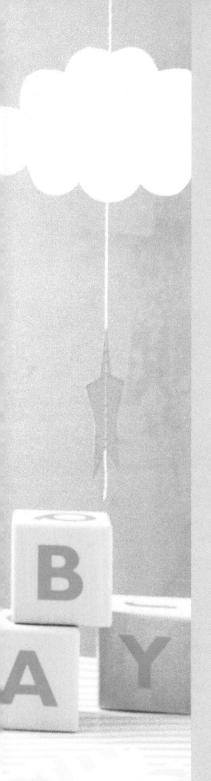

Chapter 6
SPECIAL OCCASIONS

*Baby Shower Cake
Pops, page 142*

Lemon-Lime Pound Cake

⇝ SERVES 10 ⇜

PREP TIME: **10 MINUTES** • COOK TIME: **1 HOUR 15 MINUTES**

I get excited every time I talk about my Lemon-Lime Pound Cake! It is a classic, especially here in the South, where it has been showing up at celebrations—from birthdays to baby showers—for decades. This rich, dense pound cake flavored with the bubbly lemon-lime soda plus extra lemon and lime zest and juice is always a crowd pleaser. My big secret here is that I think this cake is just as good without the glaze, so if you're pressed for time, go ahead and skip it. You can use any lemon-lime soda here, but aficionados swear that 7Up makes for the best flavor.

FOR THE CAKE

Butter and flour or cooking spray, for preparing the pan

1½ cups (3 sticks) unsalted butter, at room temperature

3 cups granulated sugar

5 large eggs, at room temperature

1 teaspoon lemon zest

1 teaspoon lime zest

1 tablespoon freshly squeezed lemon juice

1 tablespoon freshly squeezed lime juice

1 teaspoon vanilla extract

¼ teaspoon kosher salt

3 cups all-purpose flour

1 cup 7UP (or other lemon-lime soda)

FOR THE GLAZE (OPTIONAL)

1 cup confectioners' sugar

1 tablespoon freshly squeezed lemon juice

1 to 2 tablespoons 7UP (or other lemon-lime soda)

1. **To make the cake,** preheat the oven to 350°F. Coat a Bundt pan or tube pan with butter and dust it with flour, or coat it with cooking spray.
2. In a large bowl using an electric mixer or in the bowl of a stand mixer, cream together the butter and sugar on medium-high speed until pale yellow and fluffy. Add the eggs one at a time, beating after each to incorporate. Add the lemon zest, lime zest, lemon juice, lime juice, vanilla, and salt and beat to incorporate. Add 1 cup of flour and beat to incorporate. Add ½ cup of the 7UP and beat to incorporate. Repeat with the remaining flour and 7UP, ending with the flour.

3. Transfer the batter to the prepared pan. Bake for 60 to 75 minutes, until a toothpick inserted in the center comes out clean.

4. Remove the pan from the oven and let the cake cool in the pan for about 15 minutes before inverting onto a wire rack to cool completely.

5. **To make the glaze (if using),** in a small bowl stir together the confectioners' sugar, lemon juice, and 1 tablespoon of 7UP and mix until smooth. Add the remaining 7UP as needed to achieve the desired consistency.

6. Drizzle the glaze over the cake and serve at room temperature.

TECHNIQUE TIP: Be careful not to overmix the batter once you've begun adding the flour. After each flour addition, beat just until the flour is incorporated.

Red Velvet Birthday Cake

⇥ SERVES 10 ⇤

PREP TIME: **30 MINUTES** • COOK TIME: **30 MINUTES**

. . . .

*T*his recipe is dedicated to three important people in my life: me, myself, and I! It's my favorite color and my favorite flavor—red and chocolate. The cocoa-flavored cake is enhanced by the tang of buttermilk. Oh, and don't forget the silky white cream cheese frosting and its striking juxtaposition with the red-brown cake. I love it, and I know you will, too. If you make this cake, be sure to tag me on social media and say, "Happy birthday." (That's right, it's my birthday all over again anytime someone makes this cake!)

. . . .

FOR THE CAKE

Butter, for greasing the pan

3 cups cake flour

1 teaspoon baking soda

2 tablespoons unsweetened cocoa powder

½ teaspoon kosher salt

½ cup (1 stick) unsalted butter, at room temperature

2 cups granulated sugar

1 cup vegetable oil

4 large eggs, at room temperature

1 tablespoon vanilla extract

1 teaspoon distilled white vinegar

1 cup buttermilk, at room temperature

1½ teaspoons red gel food coloring

FOR THE FROSTING

½ cup (1 stick) unsalted butter, at room temperature

2 (8-ounce) packages cream cheese, at room temperature

4 to 4¼ cups confectioners' sugar

1 tablespoon milk

1½ teaspoons vanilla extract

Pinch kosher salt

. . . .

1. **To make the cake,** preheat the oven to 350°F. Coat two (9-inch) round cake pans with butter, line the pans with parchment paper, and butter the parchment paper.

2. In a large bowl, whisk together the flour, baking soda, cocoa, and salt.

3. In a separate large bowl using an electric mixer or in the bowl of a stand mixer, cream together the butter and sugar on medium-high speed for 1 minute. Add the oil, eggs, vanilla, and vinegar and beat on high for 2 minutes.

CONTINUED >>

4. With the mixer on low speed, add one-third of the dry ingredients and beat to incorporate. Add ½ cup of buttermilk and beat to incorporate. Add half of the remaining dry ingredients and beat until incorporated. Beat in the remaining ½ cup of buttermilk and then the remaining dry ingredients.

5. Add the food coloring and beat to incorporate.

6. Transfer the batter to the prepared cake pans, dividing equally. Bake for about 30 minutes, until the cakes spring back when pressed.

7. Remove the pans from the oven and set them on a wire rack to cool completely.

8. **To make the frosting,** in a large bowl using an electric mixer or in the bowl of a stand mixer, beat together the butter and cream cheese on medium-high speed until smooth. Add 4 cups of confectioners' sugar, the milk, the vanilla, and the salt and beat for about 3 minutes, gradually adding in the remaining confectioners' sugar as needed until the mixture is well combined, thick, and creamy. If the consistency isn't right, you can thicken it by beating in a bit more confectioners' sugar or thin it with a bit more milk.

9. **To assemble the cake,** start by trimming the cakes. Use a serrated knife to level the tops of the cake layers.

10. Dollop a bit of frosting on your cake platter or stand and set one of the cake layers on top, cut-side down. Top with a hearty dollop of frosting and spread it into an even layer. Place the second cake layer on top, cut-side down, and top that layer with a another hearty dollop of frosting. Smooth the frosting into an even layer. Spread frosting around the sides to cover evenly in a thick layer. Serve the cake at room temperature.

SUBSTITUTION TIP: If you don't have cake flour, you can substitute a mixture of all-purpose flour and cornstarch. Sift together 2½ cups plus 2 tablespoons of all-purpose flour with ¼ cup plus 2 tablespoons of cornstarch.

Confetti Rainbow Cake

✦ SERVES 12 ✦

PREP TIME: **1 HOUR** • COOK TIME: **ABOUT 30 MINUTES (2 BATCHES)**

*N*ews flash: You do not need a boxed mix to make a fun-filled confetti cake. I am a serious funfetti-er. I adore anything and everything to do with sprinkles, cake batter, nonpareils, and rainbow colors, and this right here is the mother of all funfetti cakes. It is made 100 percent from scratch in no time at all, and multiple people have told me it's the best cake they've EVER eaten.

FOR THE CAKE

Butter and flour or cooking spray, for preparing the pans

3¾ cups all-purpose flour

¾ teaspoon baking powder

¾ teaspoon baking soda

1 teaspoon kosher salt

1½ cups (3 sticks) unsalted butter, at room temperature

1¾ cups granulated sugar

4 large eggs, at room temperature

1 tablespoon vanilla extract

1½ cups buttermilk, at room temperature

2 egg whites, at room temperature

6 colors of gel food coloring (red, orange, yellow, green, blue, and purple)

FOR THE FROSTING

1½ cups (3 sticks) unsalted butter, at room temperature

6 cups confectioners' sugar

1 tablespoon vanilla extract

⅛ teaspoon kosher salt

4 to 6 tablespoons milk or cream

1½ cups rainbow nonpareils, for decorating

1. **To make the cake,** preheat the oven to 350°F. Butter six (6-inch cake) pans and dust them with flour, or coat them with cooking spray. Line each with a round of parchment paper and butter the parchment.

2. In a medium bowl, whisk together the flour, baking powder, baking soda, and salt.

3. In a large bowl using an electric mixer or in the bowl of a stand mixer, beat the butter on high speed for about 1 minute, until creamy and smooth. Add the sugar and beat for about 5 minutes on high speed.

4. Add the eggs one at a time, beating on medium speed after each to incorporate. Add the vanilla and beat to incorporate.

5. With the mixer running on low speed, add the dry ingredients in three batches, alternating with two batches of the buttermilk and beating after each addition just until incorporated.

CONTINUED >>

6. In a separate bowl, beat the egg whites on high speed for about 3 minutes, until they hold soft peaks. Using a rubber spatula, gently fold the beaten egg whites into the batter.

7. Divide the batter among six small bowls and add a different gel food coloring to each bowl.

8. Transfer the colored batter to the prepared pans (one color per pan). Unless you have a very large oven, you will need to bake the cakes in two batches. Bake each batch for 12 to 15 minutes, until a toothpick inserted in the center comes out clean.

9. Remove the pans from the oven and let the cakes cool for about 20 minutes before inverting them onto wire racks to cool completely.

10. **To make the frosting,** in a large bowl using an electric mixer or in the bowl of a stand mixer, cream the butter on high speed until smooth. Add the confectioners' sugar about 2 cups at a time, and beat until thick and well combined. Add the vanilla and salt and beat to incorporate. Add 4 tablespoons of milk and beat to combine. Add additional milk as needed, 1 tablespoon at a time, to achieve the right consistency.

11. **To assemble the cake,** place the red cake layer on your cake platter or cake stand and dollop some of the frosting on top. Spread the frosting into a thick, even layer. Repeat with the remaining cake layers, stacking the orange, yellow, green, blue, and purple layers in order and layering frosting in between.

12. Spread frosting all around the top and sides of the cake in a thick, even layer. Coat the top and sides of the cake with the nonpareils.

ADVANCED TIP: Add candies in the middle of your cake for a party surprise! After the cake layers have cooled, cut a hole in the middle of the red, orange, yellow, green, and blue layers with a 3-inch round cutter. Assemble the cake in the same order, with a layer of frosting between each cake layer. Before you put on the purple (uncut) layer, pour 1 to 1½ cups of M&Ms or other small candies into the hole. Top with the final layer of cake, and frost and decorate as directed.

Baby Shower Cake Pops

*T*hese pastel-colored baby shower treats are super fun and delicious! They are also perfect to use for a gender reveal, serving white candy-covered cake pops that conceal a blue or pink filling. Just take a bite to find out whether the guest of honor is expecting a boy or girl. If you want to be sassy, mix it up and put both colors inside the pops—let them keep guessing!

1 (9-by-13-inch) white cake (made from a boxed mix or from scratch, like the cake part of the Confetti Rainbow Cake on page 139), cooled to room temperature

1½ cups (3 sticks) unsalted butter, at room temperature

6 cups confectioners' sugar

1 tablespoon vanilla

⅛ teaspoon kosher salt

4 to 6 tablespoons milk or cream

Gel food coloring

Sprinkles

2 tablespoons vegetable shortening

2 (11-ounce) bags white candy melts

1. Crumble the cake into a large bowl.
2. In a large bowl using an electric mixer or in the bowl of a stand mixer, cream the butter on high speed until smooth. Add the confectioners' sugar, about 2 cups at a time, and beat until thick and well combined. Add the vanilla and salt and beat to incorporate. Add 4 tablespoons of milk and beat to combine. Add additional milk as needed to achieve the right consistency.
3. Using a rubber spatula, fold the frosting into the cake crumbs a little bit at a time. Keep adding frosting and mixing until the crumbs hold together and you can form the mixture into balls.
4. Add a few drops of gel food coloring. Use a rubber spatula to fold the coloring into the mixture until it is all evenly colored.
5. Form the mixture into 1-inch balls. You can use a small cookie scoop to form the balls or just roll the mixture in your

hands. Arrange the balls on a baking sheet. You should have about 48 cake balls. Insert a lollipop stick about halfway through each ball. Refrigerate for at least 30 minutes to firm up the cake pops.

6. Place the sprinkles in a bowl.

7. Melt the shortening in the top of a double boiler set over simmering water. Add the candy melts and stir until the candy melts are completely melted and the mixture is smooth. Pour the mixture into a drinking glass or a glass measuring cup and let cool for a few minutes before you begin dipping.

8. Dip each cake pop into the coating, completely covering the cake ball, as well as the end of the lollipop stick where it goes into the ball. Roll the cake pop to ensure that it is evenly coated and let the excess drip off into the bowl. Immediately dip the cake pop in the sprinkles, rolling to coat evenly.

9. Place each cake pop on the baking sheet, with the sticks sticking up. Once they are all coated, chill in the refrigerator for at least 1 hour to set the coating. Serve the cake pops at room temperature.

ADVANCED TIP: Instead of using sprinkles, you could use royal icing to pipe decorations on the cake pops after the coating has set.

Italian Cream Wedding Cake

⤙ SERVES 12 ⤚

PREP TIME: **40 MINUTES** • COOK TIME: **25 MINUTES**

*T*his recipe is dedicated to my best friend and one of my favorite cousins, Bernelta. She's not married, but I'm pretty sure I'll be making this very cake for her wedding one day. No one seems to know why this cake—which originated in my home state of Texas—is called Italian cream cake. It's a buttermilk-vanilla cake topped with a rich cream cheese frosting, pecans, and coconut. But really, who cares where it came from? All you need to know is that it is deee-licious.

FOR THE CAKE

Butter and flour or cooking spray, for preparing the pans

2 cups all-purpose flour

1 teaspoon baking soda

½ teaspoon kosher salt

½ cup (1 stick) unsalted butter, at room temperature

½ cup vegetable shortening

2 cups granulated sugar

5 large eggs, at room temperature, separated

1 teaspoon vanilla extract

1 cup buttermilk

½ cup coconut

1 cup pecans

FOR THE FROSTING

8 ounces cream cheese, at room temperature

4 tablespoons unsalted butter, at room temperature

4 cups confectioners' sugar

1 teaspoon vanilla extract

½ cup chopped pecans

1 cup sweetened shredded coconut

1. **To make the cake,** preheat the oven to 350°F. Coat three (9-inch) round baking pans with butter and dust with flour, or coat generously with cooking spray. Line each pan with a round of parchment paper and butter the parchment, as well.

2. In a medium bowl, whisk together the flour, baking soda, and salt.

3. In a large bowl using an electric mixer or in the bowl of a stand mixer, cream together the butter, shortening, and sugar on medium-high speed until pale yellow and fluffy. Add the egg yolks one at a time, beating after each to incorporate. Add the vanilla and beat to incorporate.

4. Add half of the dry ingredients to the wet ingredients and beat to incorporate. Add half of the buttermilk and beat to combine. Add the remaining

flour and buttermilk in separate additions, beating after each.

5. With a rubber spatula, gently fold in the coconut and pecans.

6. In a large bowl using an electric mixer or in the bowl of a stand mixer (making sure both the bowl and the beaters are clean), beat the egg whites until they form stiff peaks.

7. With a rubber spatula, gently fold the whipped egg whites into the batter.

8. Transfer the batter to the prepared cake pans, dividing equally. Bake for 23 to 25 minutes, until the top of the cakes springs back when pressed and a toothpick inserted in the center comes out clean.

9. Remove the pans from the oven and set on wire racks to cool for about 10 minutes before inverting the cakes onto the wire racks to cool completely.

10. **To make the frosting,** in a large bowl using an electric mixer or in the bowl of a stand mixer, cream together the cream cheese and butter on medium-high speed until smooth and fluffy. Add the confectioners' sugar and vanilla and beat until the mixture is well combined and a good, thick spreading consistency.

11. **To assemble the cake,** trim off the domed tops of the cake layers using a serrated knife.

12. Place the first layer, cut-side down, on your cake platter or cake stand. Dollop frosting on top and spread it into a thick, even layer. Repeat with the remaining layers.

13. Spread frosting around the sides of the cake in a thick, even layer. Coat the top and sides of the cake with the pecans and coconut.

TECHNIQUE TIP: Toast shredded coconut by spreading it out on a rimmed baking sheet and toasting in a 350°F oven for 7 to 10 minutes.

TROUBLESHOOTING TIP: If your frosting is too thick, add milk or cream, 1 tablespoon at a time, until you get the right consistency. If the frosting is too thin, add additional confectioners' sugar a couple of tablespoons at a time.

Sprinkledoodles

❖ MAKES ABOUT 24 COOKIES ❖
PREP TIME: **15 MINUTES** • COOK TIME: **12 MINUTES**

*G*iven how much I love cinnamon, it would be a travesty for me to write a baking book and not include a recipe for snickerdoodles! These soft cookies are the best way to enjoy my favorite spice because they are adorned with brightly colored sprinkles—Sprinkledoodles!

FOR THE COOKIES

1 cup (2 sticks) unsalted butter, at room temperature

¾ cup granulated sugar

½ cup brown sugar

1 large egg

2 teaspoons vanilla extract

1½ teaspoons ground cinnamon

1 teaspoon baking soda

1 teaspoon cream of tartar

½ teaspoon kosher salt

2¾ cups all-purpose flour

FOR THE COATING

⅓ cup granulated sugar

1½ teaspoons ground cinnamon

¾ cup rainbow sprinkles or nonpareils

1. **To make the cookies,** preheat the oven to 325°F and line a large baking sheet with parchment paper.

2. In a large bowl using an electric mixer or in the bowl of a stand mixer, cream together the butter and both sugars on medium speed until pale yellow and fluffy. Add the egg, vanilla, cinnamon, baking soda, cream of tartar, and salt and beat on medium speed until well combined, about 1 minute.

3. Add the flour and beat on low speed until just combined.

4. **To make the coating,** in a small bowl, stir together the sugar and cinnamon. Put the sprinkles in a separate small bowl.

5. Using a small cookie scoop or a tablespoon, scoop the dough into balls, rolling them between your palms to make them nice and round. Roll each ball first in the cinnamon-sugar mixture and then in the sprinkles, pressing to make sure the sprinkles stick. Once coated, place the cookies on the prepared baking sheet, leaving 2 inches

between them. Use the bottom of a juice glass or another container to press the cookies to about ¼-inch flat.

6. Bake for 10 to 12 minutes, until the cookies are just beginning to brown around the edges.

7. Remove the pan from the oven and let the cookies cool for a few minutes before transferring them to a wire rack to cool completely.

MAKE AHEAD TIP: You can make the dough well in advance, as it will keep in the refrigerator for up to 3 days. If you want to make it even further ahead of time, I recommend forming the dough balls but not coating them. Freeze the dough balls on a parchment-lined baking sheet and then transfer them to a resealable plastic bag and keep them in the freezer for up to 3 months. To bake, thaw them by letting them stand at room temperature for about 30 minutes, then roll them in the coatings, flatten, and bake as directed.

Someone's Been Making Whoopie . . . Pies

*I*t's funny because it's true, right? So why not have a bit of fun with your baby shower menu? Fluffy little chocolate cakes sandwich a marshmallow creme filling, which can be colored pink and baby blue for the occasion.

FOR THE CAKES

Butter, for greasing the pans

4 cups all-purpose flour

1 cup unsweetened cocoa powder

2½ teaspoons baking soda

1 teaspoon kosher salt

1 cup (2 sticks) unsalted butter, at room temperature

2 cups granulated sugar

2 large eggs

2 teaspoons vanilla extract

2 cups buttermilk

FOR THE FILLING

1 cup (2 sticks) unsalted butter, at room temperature

2½ cups confectioners' sugar

4 cups marshmallow creme

2 teaspoons vanilla extract

Red gel food coloring

Blue gel food coloring

1½ cups sweetened shredded coconut

1. **To make the cakes,** preheat the oven to 350°F and coat 2 large baking sheets with butter.

2. In a medium bowl, whisk together the flour, cocoa, baking soda, and salt.

3. In a large bowl using an electric mixer or in the bowl of a stand mixer, cream together the butter and sugar on medium-high speed until pale yellow and fluffy. Add the eggs and vanilla and beat to incorporate.

4. With the mixer on low speed, add the dry ingredients in three batches, alternating with the buttermilk in two batches, ending with the dry ingredients. Beat to incorporate after each addition. Once everything has been added, beat just until smooth.

5. Use an ice cream scooper to mound the batter, about ¼ cup per mound, on the prepared baking sheets, leaving about 2 inches in between mounds. Bake one sheet at a time for about 12 minutes, until the cakes puff up and spring back when pressed lightly.

6. Remove the pans from the oven and transfer the cakes to a wire rack to cool completely.

7. **To make the filling,** in a medium bowl using an electric mixer or in the bowl of a stand mixer, combine the butter, confectioners' sugar, marshmallow creme, and vanilla. Beat on medium speed for about 3 minutes until the mixture is smooth and thick.

8. Divide the filling into two equal portions and stir about 4 or 5 drops of red food coloring into one portion and 4 or 5 drops of blue food coloring into the other.

9. Divide the coconut into two equal portions in two small bowls. Add 2 or 3 drops of red food coloring to one bowl and 2 or 3 drops of blue food coloring to the other and toss to mix well.

10. **To assemble the whoopie pies,** dollop a heaping spoonful of pink filling on the flat side of one-fourth of the cakes and spread with a knife into an even layer. Top with an unfrosted cake, flat side toward the filling, to make a sandwich.

11. Repeat with the remaining cakes and the blue filling.

12. Press the sandwiches down so that the filling squishes all the way to the edges of the cakes and even a little bit beyond.

13. Roll the edges of the pink-filled cakes in the pink coconut so that the coconut sticks to the filling. Repeat with the blue-filled cakes and the blue coconut. Serve immediately.

SUBSTITUTION TIP: If you don't like coconut, you could use pink and blue sprinkles or sanding sugar to coat the edges instead.

Caramel Corn Brownies

⚡ MAKES 16 BROWNIES ⚡

PREP TIME: 20 MINUTES, PLUS 4 HOURS TO CHILL • COOK TIME: 35 MINUTES

*C*aramel corn or brownies—how can you possibly choose? Listen to what I'm saying: You don't have to! Put that sticky, crunchy caramel corn on top of gooey, fudgy brownies and decorate it all with a chocolate drizzle. All I can say is YUM!

FOR THE BROWNIES

Butter and flour or cooking spray, for preparing the pan

1 cup all-purpose flour

¼ teaspoon baking powder

½ teaspoon kosher salt

5 ounces bittersweet chocolate, chopped

½ cup (1 stick) unsalted butter, cut into pieces

1 cup granulated sugar

1 teaspoon vanilla extract

2 large eggs

FOR THE CARAMEL CORN

¾ cup granulated sugar

⅓ cup light corn syrup

3 tablespoons water

Pinch kosher salt

⅓ cup heavy (whipping) cream

1 teaspoon vanilla extract

2 cups popped popcorn

FOR THE TOPPING

2 ounces dark chocolate, chopped

1. **To make the brownies,** preheat the oven to 350°F. Coat a 9-inch square baking pan with butter and dust with flour, or coat with cooking spray.

2. In a medium bowl, whisk together the flour, baking powder, and salt.

3. In the top of a double boiler, combine the chocolate and butter and heat over simmering water, stirring frequently, until the chocolate is completely melted and the mixture is smooth (or melt it in the microwave in 30-second intervals, stirring in between).

   Remove from the heat and let cool for about 10 minutes. Stir in the sugar and vanilla.

4. Add the eggs one at a time, beating after each addition to incorporate. Add the dry ingredients and beat just to incorporate.

5. Transfer the batter to the prepared pan and bake for 30 to 35 minutes, until the top is shiny and a toothpick inserted in the center comes out clean. Place the pan on a wire rack while you make the caramel corn.

6. **To make the caramel corn,** in a medium saucepan, combine the sugar, corn syrup, water, and salt over medium heat. Bring the mixture to a boil and cook, stirring constantly, until the sugar dissolves completely. Reduce the heat to low and let the mixture simmer, without stirring, for about 10 minutes, until it turns golden brown. Remove the pan from the heat and stir in the cream and vanilla. (Note that the mixture will bubble up and release steam when you add the cream, so use caution.)

7. Stir in the popcorn and pour the mixture over the brownies in the pan, quickly spreading it into an even layer.

8. **To make the topping,** melt the chocolate in a double boiler over simmering water (or in the microwave in 30-second intervals, stirring in between).

9. Drizzle the chocolate over the popcorn using a spoon or fork or by putting it into a resealable plastic bag and snipping off the corner to make a piping bag.

10. Cover and refrigerate for at least 4 hours to set the chocolate topping and the caramel corn layer.

11. Cut the brownies into squares and serve cold or at room temperature.

TECHNIQUE TIP: Use a parchment paper sling to line the brownie pan to make it easy to lift the whole thing out of the pan to serve.

Cookies-and-Cream Ice Cream Cake

✦ SERVES 8 ✦

PREP TIME: 15 MINUTES, PLUS 5 HOURS TO FREEZE

My brother Khalill is obsessed with all things cookies-and-cream, so I make this cake for his birthday every year. Ice cream cakes are great for all sorts of celebrations—birthdays, picnics, backyard barbecues, and more. They are easy to make, and it's a fun mix-and-match flavor combination. Because it's for Khalill, this recipe combines cookies-and-cream ice cream with chocolate sandwich cookies, hot fudge sauce, and whipped topping, but you can substitute any flavors you like.

1 package (20 cookies) chocolate sandwich cookies, crushed, divided

4 tablespoons unsalted butter, melted

½ gallon cookies-and-cream ice cream, softened

2 cups (16 ounces) hot fudge sauce

1 (8-ounce) tub frozen whipped topping, thawed

1. Line a 9-by-5-inch loaf pan with a parchment paper sling.

2. In a bowl, stir together the cookie crumbs, reserving ¼ cup for the topping, and melted butter until thoroughly moistened. Press the mixture into an even layer on the bottom of the prepared pan.

3. Spoon the ice cream on top of the crust and spread it into an even layer. Freeze for at least 2 hours.

4. Warm the fudge sauce a bit in the microwave so that it is pourable, then pour it over the ice cream in the pan. Freeze for 1 hour more.

5. Spread the whipped topping over the top of the fudge sauce, sprinkle the reserved cookie crumbs over the top, and freeze for 2 more hours.

6. To serve, lift the ice cream cake out of the loaf pan using the parchment paper sling and slice.

SUBSTITUTION TIP: You can mix and match the cookies, ice cream, and sauce here. For the crust, you can use graham crackers, chocolate wafer cookies, gingersnaps, or any crunchy cookie you like. Choose an ice cream flavor to complement your cookies. Stick with hot fudge sauce, or use caramel or butterscotch sauce instead.

Unicorn Cookies

⇥ MAKES ABOUT 24 COOKIES ⇤

PREP TIME: 1 HOUR, PLUS 1 HOUR TO CHILL AND OVERNIGHT TO SET

COOK TIME: 12 MINUTES

. . . .

I promise you that these magical, mythical creatures will delight every single person you serve them to. I wanted to use this recipe to show how you can make sugar cookies in all sorts of guises without having to buy a new cookie cutter shape every time. All you need here is a round cookie cutter and your creativity!

. . . .

FOR THE COOKIES

3 cups all-purpose flour

¾ teaspoon baking powder

¼ teaspoon kosher salt

1 cup (2 sticks) unsalted butter, at room temperature

1 cup granulated sugar

1 large egg

1 tablespoon milk

1 teaspoon vanilla extract

FOR THE ICING

3 cups confectioners' sugar

1½ tablespoons meringue powder

4 to 6 tablespoons water

½ teaspoon vanilla extract

FOR DECORATING

White fondant

Black food marker

Gold edible mist spray

½ cup white candy melts

Snowflakes, sugar flowers, and pearl sprinkles

. . . .

1. **To make the cookies,** in a medium bowl, whisk together the flour, baking powder, and salt.

2. In a large bowl using an electric mixer or in the bowl of a stand mixer, cream together the butter and sugar on medium-high speed until pale yellow and fluffy. Add the egg, milk, and vanilla and beat to combine.

3. With the mixer running on low speed, gradually add the dry ingredients, beating until the mixture is well combined and begins to pull away from the sides of the bowl. Divide the dough into two equal portions.

4. Roll out one of the dough portions between two pieces of parchment paper to ¼-inch thickness. Remove the top piece of parchment and slide the

CONTINUED >>

remaining piece of parchment onto a baking sheet. Use a 2-inch round cutter to cut out cookies.

5. Carefully remove the excess cookie dough from around the cutouts. (You can reroll this and use it to make more cookies.) Cover the pan with plastic wrap and chill for 1 hour.

6. Preheat the oven to 350°F.

7. Bake the cookies for 10 to 12 minutes, until the edges are just starting to brown a bit.

8. **To make the icing,** in a large bowl using an electric mixer or in the bowl of a stand mixer, combine the confectioners' sugar and meringue powder. Add 4 tablespoons of water and the vanilla and beat on low speed to combine. Add additional water as needed to achieve the right consistency. The icing should be fairly thick and very smooth. Raise the speed of the mixer gradually and beat until the icing is thick and glossy.

9. Fill a piping bag fitted with a small, round tip half full with icing. Pipe a thin outline of icing around the outside edge of each cookie.

10. Transfer any remaining icing back to the bowl. Add about 1 teaspoon of water to the icing to thin it, stirring to mix well. Add additional water as needed to get it to the consistency of a thick syrup. Return the thinned icing to the piping bag and flood the top of the cookie inside the icing outline. You can use a toothpick to spread the icing into any missed spots.

11. Once all the cookies are iced, let them sit out at room temperature, uncovered, overnight. The icing will dry and harden.

12. **To make the decorations,** on the same day you ice your cookies, pinch off a piece of fondant and roll it into a rope about 1½ inches long, tapering at one end. Make a second rope the same size and twist the two together, pinching at the tapered ends to seal them. Cut off the bottom of the horn with a knife. Repeat to make as many horns as you have cookies. Let the horns dry overnight.

13. Roll out some of the fondant to about ⅛-inch thickness. Use a very small teardrop or triangle-shaped fondant

cutter to cut out two ears for each cookie. Let them dry.

14. Once the icing is completely dry, use the food marker to draw eyelashes onto the cookies.

15. Spray the horns with the gold mist. To paint the ears, spray some of the gold mist into a small bowl and use a small food-safe brush to paint the mist onto the inside of the ear cutouts.

16. Melt the candy melts in a small bowl in the microwave by heating on 50 percent power in 30-second intervals, stirring in between, until completely melted and smooth.

17. Use a small food-safe brush to brush the melted candy melt onto the bottom of the horns and stick them onto the cookies. Do the same with the ears, attaching one ear on either side of the horn.

18. Use the candy melts to attach snowflakes, flowers, and pearls to the unicorns.

TECHNIQUE TIP: For a simpler approach, use a unicorn-shaped cookie cutter to cut out your cookies and then ice, paint, and decorate them accordingly.

Peanut Butter Chocolate Graduation Caps

✤ MAKES 16 ✤

PREP TIME: 45 MINUTES, PLUS 20 MINUTES TO CHILL

M aking filled chocolate candies seems like a big undertaking, but I promise you it is easier than you think. These adorable cap-and-gown confections are a great way to celebrate your newest graduate.

FOR THE CHOCOLATE SHELLS

16 ounces dark chocolate, chopped

FOR THE FILLING

½ cup creamy peanut butter

½ cup confectioners' sugar

1½ tablespoons unsalted butter, at room temperature

½ teaspoon kosher salt

FOR DECORATING

3 ounces white modeling chocolate

1. **To make the chocolate shells,** place the chocolate in a microwave-safe bowl and heat it in the microwave on 50 percent power in 30-second intervals, stirring in between, until the chocolate is completely melted and the mixture is smooth.

2. Use a digital instant-read thermometer to track the temperature of the chocolate as it cools. Once it is between 86°F and 93°F, it is ready to be put into a mold.

3. Using a silicone mold, create 16 chocolate domes by brushing a thin layer of the melted chocolate into each cavity.

4. Let stand at room temperature or, to speed the process, in the refrigerator for a few minutes, until the chocolate hardens.

5. **To make the filling,** stir together the peanut butter, confectioners' sugar, butter, and salt until smooth.

6. Spoon or pipe the peanut butter filling into the chocolate shells, leaving a bit of space at the top. Chill in the refrigerator for a few minutes.

7. Spoon or pipe a layer of chocolate over the filling to seal it off. Chill in the refrigerator until firm. Pop the chocolates out of the molds.

CONTINUED >>

8. Pour the remaining chocolate (you may need to rewarm it) into an 8-inch square pan to about ⅛ inch thick. Let it stand for a few minutes to firm up a bit but not become totally hard. Use a sharp knife or a square cookie cutter to cut out 16 squares, about 2 by 2 inches. Let the squares stand or refrigerate them until they harden.

9. Reheat any remaining chocolate and use a small food-safe brush to brush it onto the rounded part of the filled chocolates and the under part of the chocolate squares to attach the squares to the filled chocolates.

10. **To make the decorations,** roll the white modeling chocolate into thin ropes and cut to create "strings." Attach a clump of strings to the top of each chocolate square.

11. Pinch off a small piece of modeling chocolate and form it into a ball. Press the ball on top of the end of the tassels where they attach to the top of the hat to seal the tassels to the hat. Repeat until all the hats have tassels.

Garlic-Parmesan Knots

✦ MAKES 16 KNOTS ✦

PREP TIME: 20 MINUTES, PLUS 1 HOUR TO RISE • COOK TIME: 12 MINUTES

I looooove garlic, and these Garlic-Parmesan Knots are loaded with it. Serve them alongside pasta or any dish with a sauce that begs to be sopped up with bread.

FOR THE KNOTS

1⅓ cups warm water (105°F to 110°F)

1 tablespoon active dry yeast

2 tablespoons granulated sugar

3½ cups all-purpose flour

1 teaspoon kosher salt

Nonstick cooking spray, for greasing

FOR THE GARLIC BUTTER TOPPING

4 tablespoons unsalted butter, melted

6 garlic cloves, finely minced

2 tablespoons olive oil

2 tablespoons finely chopped fresh flat-leaf parsley

½ teaspoon flaky sea salt

¼ cup freshly grated Parmesan cheese

1. **To make the knots,** in a large bowl using an electric mixer or in the bowl of a stand mixer, combine the water, yeast, and sugar and stir to mix. Let stand for 10 minutes, until frothy.

2. Add the flour and salt and beat on low speed until the mixture comes together into a sticky dough. Raise the mixer speed to high and beat for about 3 minutes, until the dough is smooth.

3. Coat a large bowl with cooking spray and transfer the dough to it, turning to coat it with the oil. Cover the dough and let it sit in a warm place (like your kitchen countertop or inside the oven with only the light turned on) until it doubles in size, about 1 hour.

4. Preheat the oven to 400°F and coat a large baking sheet with cooking spray.

5. Cut the dough in quarters and then cut each quarter into quarters to make 16 pieces. Roll each piece into an 8-inch-long rope. Loop the rope into a knot and press the ends together to seal them. Set the knots on the prepared baking sheet with 2 inches in between them.

6. **To make the topping,** stir together the butter, garlic, oil, parsley, salt, and cheese in a bowl. Using a pastry brush, brush the mixture onto the knots, covering the entire surface of each.

7. Bake for 10 to 12 minutes, until the knots are golden brown. Serve warm or store at room temperature.

Homemade Pretzels

*I*f you have shied away from making homemade bread, this is the perfect recipe to get you started because it is crazy easy. These pretzels are bready and salty and perfect for dunking in mustard, ranch dressing, or any dipping sauce you like. You can even take these in a sweet direction by topping them with cinnamon sugar instead of salt.

1½ cups warm water (105°F to 110°F)

1 packet (2¼ teaspoons) instant yeast

1 tablespoon granulated sugar

1 teaspoon kosher salt

1 tablespoon unsalted butter, melted

3¾ to 4 cups all-purpose flour, plus more for dusting

Nonstick cooking spray, for greasing the bowl

½ cup baking soda

4 cups boiling water

Coarse sea salt, for sprinkling

1. In a large bowl using an electric mixer or in the bowl of a stand mixer, combine the water and yeast. Let stand for a few minutes, until frothy. Add the sugar, salt, and butter and whisk to combine. Add the flour 1 cup at a time, mixing well between additions. If the dough is still sticky after adding 3¾ cups of flour, add the remaining ¼ cup of flour 1 tablespoon at a time. You may not need all of the flour. When it is ready, it should be smooth, elastic, and no longer sticky.

2. On a lightly floured work surface, knead the dough for 3 to 4 minutes. If you are using a stand mixer, you can knead it with the dough hook. Form the dough into a ball.

3. Coat a large bowl lightly with cooking spray and add the dough, turning it to coat with the oil. Cover and let stand in a warm, draft-free spot in your kitchen until it doubles in size, about 1 hour.

4. Preheat the oven to 400°F and line two large baking sheets with parchment

paper. In a large bowl, combine the baking soda and boiling water.

5. Divide the dough into 12 pieces. Roll each piece into a rope about 8 inches long. Form the ropes into pretzel shapes by first making them into a circle and then twisting the top part of the circle down and attaching it to the bottom.

6. Dunk each pretzel into the baking soda solution and then place it onto one of the prepared baking sheets. Sprinkle the coarse salt over the tops of the pretzels.

7. Bake in two batches, until the pretzels are golden brown, 12 to 15 minutes. Serve warm.

ADVANCED TIP: Make a honey mustard dipping sauce to top off your pretzels. Combine equal parts Dijon mustard and honey, and stir to mix well.

MEASUREMENT CONVERSIONS

VOLUME EQUIVALENTS (LIQUID)

US STANDARD	US STANDARD (OUNCES)	METRIC (APPROXIMATE)
2 tablespoons	1 fl. oz.	30 mL
¼ cup	2 fl. oz.	60 mL
½ cup	4 fl. oz.	120 mL
1 cup	8 fl. oz.	240 mL
1½ cups	12 fl. oz.	355 mL
2 cups or 1 pint	16 fl. oz.	475 mL
4 cups or 1 quart	32 fl. oz.	1 L
1 gallon	128 fl. oz.	4 L

OVEN TEMPERATURES

FAHRENHEIT (F)	CELSIUS (C) (APPROXIMATE)
250°	120°
300°	150°
325°	165°
350°	180°
375°	190°
400°	200°
425°	220°
450°	230°

VOLUME EQUIVALENTS (DRY)

US STANDARD	METRIC (APPROXIMATE)
⅛ teaspoon	0.5 mL
¼ teaspoon	1 mL
½ teaspoon	2 mL
¾ teaspoon	4 mL
1 teaspoon	5 mL
1 tablespoon	15 mL
¼ cup	59 mL
⅓ cup	79 mL
½ cup	118 mL
⅔ cup	156 mL
¾ cup	177 mL
1 cup	235 mL
2 cups or 1 pint	475 mL
3 cups	700 mL
4 cups or 1 quart	1 L

WEIGHT EQUIVALENTS

US STANDARD	METRIC (APPROXIMATE)
½ ounce	15 g
1 ounce	30 g
2 ounces	60 g
4 ounces	115 g
8 ounces	225 g
12 ounces	340 g
16 ounces or 1 pound	455 g

RESOURCES

AmeriColor: AmericolorCorp.com

Ateco: AtecoUSA.com

Borderlands Bakery: BorderlandsBakery.com

Cut It Out Cutters: CutItOutCutters.com

Crumbs Cutters: CrumbsCutters.com

Fat Daddio's: FatDaddios.com

Frosted by Malek Binns: FrostedByMalekBinns.com

KaleidaCuts: KaleidaCuts.com

KitchenAid: KitchenAid.com

SheyB Designs: SheyB.com

The Sugar Art: TheSugarArt.com

Wilton: Wilton.com

INDEX

ACKNOWLEDGMENTS

OMG, have we arrived at the end?! I want to ride again! It is still so surreal that this is my cookbook and my name is on the cover! Out of all my life's dreams and desires, never would I have thought that I would be adding the title "author" to my résumé. I am so honored and humbled, and I have to praise some special people who made this possible. I want to personally shout them out to express my deep gratitude and honor them. *Cue the waterworks.*

Thank you to my outstanding mother, Casika, for instilling that entrepreneurial spirit in me when I was 6 years old. I will never forget those words that inspire me every day: "You can be whatever you put your mind to and still be more than that."

Thank you to my amazing grandmother, Icilma, for being one of my biggest supporters and pushing me every day. Thanks for being the inspiration for me to try new things.

To my godmothers, Aunt Pat—for being one of my baking inspirations and sponsoring most of my baking equipment—and Aunt Pet—for always motivating me with life advice and for letting me borrow your oven and kitchen on those stressful baking nights.

Thank you to Olivia Robinson, a true friend, who has sparked the cake decorator in me. Thanks for making me cakes as a child and always teaching me cake lessons to prepare for the cake world. You are always the one I can go to about baking. Thanks for the unlimited phone calls and countless meetups.

My editor and the creative mastermind, Rebecca Markley, played a huge part in creating this book. Thanks for putting up with me and my crazy ideas. I am so grateful to know your awesome spirit and for your help making this experience worthwhile. Special thanks to my writer, Robin Donovan, who helped create the recipes and transformed them into reality. I don't know what I would've done without you both.

To my Instagram followers, this book is for you guys. You are who made this blessing happen the most. This is for each and every follow, like, share, repost, and comment that I received. Without any of those, this opportunity wouldn't have happened. Thanks for rocking with your boy.

I'd also like to extend my thanks to all my family, friends, and inspirations who have given me guidance over the years. Last but not least, I thank my haters, from my past to my future. Thanks for pushing me to be more determined and to strive for success. I always say that without haters, you are not doing anything right.

ABOUT THE AUTHOR

Malek Binns is the founder and operator of FROSTED by Malek Binns and its brother company, Sprinkled by Malek. He graduated from Le Cordon Bleu, where he specialized in baking and patisserie. He's a sucker for sweets—they're all he thinks about—especially gummy bears. When he is not baking, he can be found cracking jokes, dancing, or having fun on social media @frostedbymalekbinns. He resides in Houston, Texas.

CPSIA information can be obtained
at www.ICGtesting.com
Printed in the USA
JSHW021907090720
6577JS00002B/27